To my children

Whatever it is you say I am, I am not.
Whatever it is you want from me, I will give
Whatever it is you take from me, you can take
What is it you can do to me?
The worst thing you can do is kill me
After that I won't care,
I am still free.

MARTIN CAHILL, NOVEMBER 1988

Martin Cahill,
My Father

Martin Cahill,
My Father

FRANCES CAHILL

**NEW
ISLAND**

MARTIN CAHILL, MY FATHER
First published 2007
by New Island
2 Brookside
Dundrum Road
Dublin 14
www.newisland.ie

ISBN 978-1-905494-75-0

British Library Cataloguing in Publication Data. A CIP catalogue
record for this book is available from the British Library.

Typeset by TypeIT, Dublin
Cover design by Inka Hagen
Printed in the UK by Cox & Wyman

10 9 8 7 6 5 4 3 2 1

Contents

Timeline

23 May 1949: Martin Cahill is born to Paddy and Agnes Cahill.

1959: First criminal record, aged 10.

1961: First criminal conviction.

1965: Sent to Daingean Reformatory School.

1967: Released from Daingean.

March 1968: Marries Frances Lawless.

August 1968: Martin Cahill Jnr is born.

November 1969: Frances Cahill is born.

1970: First prison sentence. Four years for receiving stolen property.

February 1973: Christopher Cahill is born.

1974: Charged in relation to Quinnsworth robbery.

1977: Second prison sentence. Four years for possession of stolen property.

1980: Released from Mountjoy.

February 1980: Emma Cahill is born.

1980–81: Family moves from Hollyfield to Kevin Street.

27 July 1983: Thomas O'Connor and Sons jewellery factory in Harold's Cross, Dublin is robbed of £2 million worth of goods, which Martin Cahill was widely blamed for.

1983: Family moves to Cowper Downs.

May 1984: Martin stands trial for robbery. He is acquitted.

May 1986: Russborough House robbery wherein paintings worth £30 million were stolen from the Beit Collection.

October 1986: Luke Cahill is born.

1988: Tango Squad surveillance begins.

February 1988: Airing of **Today Tonight** programme on crime in Dublin's gangland, after which Martin became the subject of increased garda and media scrutiny.

June 1988: Sent to Spike Island prison in Cork to serve four months for failing to enter a bond to keep the peace.

November 1993: National Irish Bank CEO Jim Lacey, his wife and children and their babysitter are kidnapped. Subsequent investigations revealed major tax evasion scandals in the Irish banking industry.

18 August 1994: Martin Cahill is shot dead at age forty-five.

Acknowledgements

First and foremost, I would like to thank my parents, Martin and Frances Cahill, for giving me a loving and caring childhood like no other. For this, I am eternally grateful.

For my publisher, Edwin, and my editor, Deirdre Nolan, who were kind and caring and brave enough to let real people's stories be told.

For my friend Ger, who gave me that much-needed kick up the arse, and Eddie Cahill, who made me realise why I was writing about my father and who is still very much winning the battle.

And lastly, to my family – my children, to whom I dedicate this book, and to my husband Mark, without whom nothing would be possible.

Introduction
What Will Be, Will Be

On 18 August 1994, my father, Martin Cahill, was murdered.

He was killed with a handgun, shot several times in the neck and chest. My family was told that the murderer (or murderers) were white, professional assassins following IRA instructions to get rid of this man once and for all. The hidden men of the Irish Republican Army were tired of his arrogance and his disobedience towards them and decided that his time had come. 'Anyway, he must have known it was coming,' one senior member of the gardaí nonchalantly put it at the time.

My father had conjured up quite a reputation for himself. Rather, I should say the media did a terrific job portraying him as 'The General', public enemy number one, as some of the less talented and unoriginal journalists would write in their hungry little columns. They all had livings to earn, and this guy sold newspapers. He wore a hood, for God's sake. He seemed to outwit the entire Irish police force. He was even capable of disappearing before your very eyes. Some said he was like a mythical figure, a folk hero, a loveable rogue, a modern-day Robin Hood. On the

other hand, he was also compared to such people as Al
Capone and John Gotti, known in some circles as a
ruthless hardened criminal who would nail you to the
floor as quick as look at you. The newspaper-buying
public were hungry for something – a bit of gossip,
maybe – and the real gangsters in the country needed
the heat taken off them, didn't they? And yes, Martin
was a colourful character with a dangerous dark side
that walked between the shadows. The General fit the
bill. Plus, what else could brighten up the Sunday
morning papers? Certainly not boring politicians and
sexual abuse cases. The scope was limitless; stories
could run and run. It was tabloid heaven. But it all
ended that sunny Thursday afternoon.

*

During his life and after his death, Martin Cahill has
been described as a conniving professional thief and
armed robber; a person who attempted many murders
and carried out brutal, tortuous punishments; a
caricature of a man who single-handedly pulled the
wool over the eyes of the entire Irish police force and
led them through years of frustrated, hand-tied
impotence in bringing him to justice. His reputation
as a ruthless master criminal was fuelled by gardaí
hearsay and tabloid journalism.

But everything Martin did, he did just to get back
at the gardaí, or to annoy them or embarrass them.
He had no respect for them whatsoever. He thought

they were all arseholes and he called them mutts, his favourite term for them. To him they were all idiots, buffoons, and they didn't need any help from anybody in proving how ridiculous and stupid they were sometimes. To put it another way, it didn't take much for him to run circles around them. Everything became a game, and everything he ever did was part of this game – he wouldn't let them get away with anything. But with some of his brothers often locked up, he had to fight his battle alone for many years.

When he died, a lot of Ireland's so-called right-minded people said one big good riddance to a bad lot while hypocritically turning a blind eye to people such as Charles Haughey, one of the biggest gangsters our country was unfortunate enough to put our trust in, not to mention the now-exposed abusive order that is the Catholic Church. The gardaí have also repeatedly been proven to be corrupt (remember the McBrearty brothers in Donegal?). Yet of all the crimes my father was alleged to have committed, he was never even arrested in connection with half of them and was never charged with many of the offences he was supposed to have committed. 'Lack of evidence,' I hear you say. I say it was a lack of human rights, of civil rights, of constitutional rights, of democracy. Innocent until proven guilty? Not in this country. Most of the material that has been published about my father has mainly been sourced from the gardaí and it is a biased, vindictive, largely fictional account of a myth, a myth that demonised my father in the eyes of Irish society.

I didn't decide to write about my father to put the record straight or to dismiss the contents of some of the books and movies that have been made about his life. Some of the stories I have found to be amusing, others slightly offensive. Other times I have been left bewildered about the way the media has the power to turn the general public into an angry lynch mob. After his murder, RTÉ's **Late Late Show** had the audience practically saluting his killers, one comment being, 'His death was appropriate.' Appropriate? How very Christian.

*

My father's criminal record contains some offences committed during his childhood and another two convictions during the 1970s, one for possession of stolen property and another conviction for a stolen car. What other books and movies about his life document about him is complete hearsay and gardaí innuendo. I cannot escape the fact that it appears he was involved in criminal activity, but this is not what this book is about. I aim to give a true account of what life was like living with Martin Cahill. It would be hypocritical of me to suggest my father must have been guilty of the crimes that he supposedly committed, as I am a firm believer in the presumption of innocence for every citizen of a democratic society.

I am writing this book from my perspective as I was growing up and what I witnessed and lived through, what I believed my father to be and what he meant to me and my family. I am telling my father's story so that my children and their children will be proud to say, 'Remember Martin Cahill? He was my grandfather.' But more than anything else, I want to give a small piece of him – what he was really like, his humour, his individuality, his remarkable short life filled with optimism and with hopes for a brighter tomorrow – for myself.

*

There has never been a thorough investigation into my father's murder. From the day he died till now, not one member of An Garda Síochána has spoken to or interviewed any member of my family in connection with his murder. 'That's strange,' you might say. 'Aren't most murders carried out by people the victim knows? Surely they must have at least asked what he was doing that fateful morning leading up to his death.' No. The newspapers seemed to know it all anyway and it was an open and shut case in the eyes of the law – the IRA did it, thank you very much, we don't need to investigate this any further. Anyway, they did us all a favour. On the six o'clock news that evening, a senior member of the gardaí said, 'He was a bad character, but a person has been murdered and we are following a definite line of enquiry.' Sadly, that was not to be.

The people who took his life that day may still be around. They may be dead themselves. They may be picking their kids up from school or they may be preparing to take another person's life. Who knows? The world is plagued with people who care little for the value of life, people who don't even flinch when confronted with human tragedy. But what will be, will be. Maybe they will answer to a higher power in the end. Maybe we all will.

— Part I
The War Begins

Chapter 1
The War Begins

It all began in that damn field.

Martin and his brothers Eddie and John and a few of their friends would spend their days messing about, climbing and diving off walls and doing what all the other ten- and eleven-year-olds were doing. That day, they were on their wall at the back of their house, which bordered the GAA field. They never went near the other side of the GAA pitch, so the owners left the lads alone in their little corner, playing their little boy games. That day, the grass in the field had been cut and was piled into the corner where Martin and his brothers were playing. This was great fun – all the boys piled the grass up high and began diving off the wall into the soft, heavenly smelling grass below. Martin saw the police car pull up and the copper got out and eyed the boys, who at this stage stopped jumping off the wall and just stood there, staring back at the big policeman.

Martin stood on the wall. It was his turn. He smiled and dove into the mound of grass. He looked at the policeman, defying him, and in that moment, the course of his whole life would change. He turned and hopped back up on the wall to go again when the policeman grabbed him by the ankle, pulled him off the wall and dragged him by the legs into the car.

And so it began. In the eyes of the gardaí and society, he was now a criminal.

He now had a record, at the age of ten. They had him where they wanted him: 'You're a criminal now, you belong to us, to the state. We now tell you what to do. You're ours. Now sit in that corner and shut the fuck up!'

The war had begun.

That was the start of what was to become a lifelong battle with An Garda Síochána, the Irish police force. From then on, he was cornered. His choice was to either stay in that corner and do as he was told or come out fighting. He chose the latter. He and his brothers were only a bunch of kids, but the battle lines had already been drawn.

*

Martin's dream in life was to become a sailor. He wanted to follow in the footsteps of the men of his family, who were all naval people. His father was a lighthouse keeper and young Martin loved the ocean and everything about it. When he was fifteen, he went up to Belfast to apply to the British Navy for a position, but the childish game of jumping into piles of grass had turned into a criminal record for malicious damage. There was no way he was going to be accepted into the Royal Navy with this black mark on his character. His dreams were crushed then and there.

He headed back to Dublin after this rejection and contemplated his future. Where was he to go? What factory would even take him now? He was fucked. He knew what lay ahead – he was at the mercy of every single garda in the country. No one was going to take him seriously now. He and his brothers – who by now had started to get into trouble for skipping school – were consigned to being dole fodder, wasters, a league of shadows whose opinions meant nothing to anyone. But Martin said no. His plans for a naval career may have been destroyed, but there wasn't a chance of them destroying his spirit.

They would not allow themselves to be pushed into this category without a fight. They would stand up to authority with a zeal no one had ever encountered before.

*

My father, Martin Joseph Cahill, was born on 23 May 1949. He was born into a family that grew by the year, as was the norm in those days before contraception, when the Catholic Church held a firm grip on the Irish conscience. He was the second child born to Patrick (Paddy) and Agnes Cahill, their second boy, named after an uncle who emigrated to Canada.

When Agnes Sheehan met Paddy Cahill, he was working on the docks in Dublin. They fell in love, a love that was to last until they both died months apart in 1983. Agnes's family wasn't very pleased with her choice of husband and she lost touch with them, most of whom emigrated to Canada and Australia. Years later, she was reunited with her sisters and even visited one of them in Canada; her stories of Niagara Falls were intriguing to her grandchildren, most of whom had never been outside Dublin.

Agnes was a beauty, with black hair that tumbled over her shoulders, huge dark eyes and full red lips. She always cared about her appearance, even though she was pregnant most of the time. A fluent Irish speaker and a devout nationalist, she had huge sympathy for the Catholics in Northern Ireland. She wasn't a rebel or an activist, but in her quiet way she taught her children about Ireland's past and the Irish struggle against the British. One of her most prized possessions was an ancient cloak. She said this cloak had been handed down over centuries and originally came from a High King of Ireland. We never knew if it was authentic or not, but one day the cloak was gone. She said she had donated it to a museum, as she didn't want it to be lost over the years.

She loved everything Irish – the language, the people, the poetry – though she despised the Catholic Church. She was of the old stock that knew the priests never went hungry in the Famine and she held a firm grudge against them. However, she was a very gentle woman who never had a bad word to say about ordinary people and she was never known to gossip. She had come from a middle-class upbringing and her parents were shopkeepers.

Martin's mother had a huge impact on his developing attitude towards all authority. She would sit for hours and tell the children stories about Trevelyan and other well-known characters from the Famine era. She was determined to educate her children and make them wise to people who would do them harm or try to manipulate them in some way. When the other children would run off to play, Martin would always hang back, eager to hear more of her stories.

Agnes and Paddy were honest, hardworking people whose main aim in life was to raise their children as well as they could, and Paddy's focus was on putting food on the table for his fast-growing clan. Their two-up, two-down house at 210 Captain's Road in Crumlin was modern compared to many of the tenements that housed working-class Dubliners in the grim 1950s. Agnes had twenty-one births altogether; fifteen of the children survived (eight boys and seven girls). As was common then, the men of the family often took refuge in the local boozer to escape the noise and cleaning and cooking of family life, and Paddy enjoyed the after-work pint of Guinness in the dockers' pub. He was a good-natured sort, a dedicated father and a loving husband who never raised a hand to the children, which was all extremely rare in those days. He and Aggie, as he called her, had a loving relationship. Even though they had no money, they had plenty of love and life was lived one day at a time.

Martin got his gentleness from his father and his wisdom from his mother. 'You have to have courage in you, stand up for yourselves,' she would tell her young family. She loved all of her children with a tenderness rarely seen today. She accepted her family for who they were and she idiolised Martin until the day she died.

When Agnes died of breast cancer in 1983, Paddy followed her a few months later from a heart attack. He'd never suffered from heart trouble in his life. We said he died from a broken heart.

When Paddy died, Martin and his brothers carried his coffin all the way from the funeral parlour to the church in Ballyfermot (Ballyfermot was where the Corporation moved the Cahill family after leaving Hollyfield). Normally a hearse would be used, but Martin and his brothers were so proud of Paddy, they carried him on their shoulders the whole way. Hundreds of people lined the streets of Ballyfermot, where the family had been greatly respected.

My father took their deaths very hard. I don't think there was anyone in the world he cared for more than his parents.

*

The family were never practising Catholics. Martin would eye the priest suspiciously when he called to the house with his little contributions envelope. Agnes would never let him inside the door, the priest muttering, 'God bless now,' as he left empty handed. Agnes would say to Martin as she closed the door, 'We have little enough money for ourselves and that bleeder wants more legs of lamb in his freezer. Never trust a priest, sweetheart.' Even though this attitude kept the family at arm's length from the other neighbours, Martin made friends easily and the local boys looked up to him for his calmness and level headedness. Even as a young boy, he had the head of someone much older and much wiser than his years.

Paddy could only scratch his head in wonder when young Martin came home one evening with a large sack of frozen cuts of the best meat they had ever – or rather, never – seen. Agnes quizzed Martin about where he could have got this feast as they stood around the kitchen table.

'Son, where did these come from? Did ye rob them, Martin? Tell me, son.'

'Ah, Mam, come on, cook that one, it's melted,' he smiled. Agnes looked at Paddy, who was holding up a meaty leg of fine Irish lamb.

'Stick it on the fire, Aggie, we are eating lamb tonight!' Paddy laughed.

Agnes pulled Martin close to her as she took the meat to the sink. 'Martin, I don't want you getting into trouble, do ye hear me, son? Promise me now you'll keep out of trouble. Promise me, love. No good ever comes from robbin'.'

Martin smiled as he kissed her on the cheek. 'I promise, Mam. Now cook that, will ye? I can taste it already.'

That night, the parish priest cursed the culprit to high heaven as he stared angrily into his empty freezer. He eyed the window in the larder, opened only about a foot. What little bleeder got through that, he no doubt wondered.

Martin's neighbours all ate well that week – Agnes had sent him out to distribute the fast-thawing feast. This was one of Martin's first defiant acts against authority, at eleven years of age. Martin stole the priest's meat because he wanted to annoy the pompous man who had looked down his nose at him when he knew that Agnes wasn't coming across with the shilling for the Church collection, judging him and his 'sort', people who raised their heads above the suffocating shrouds of the Church. The priest saw that, and he saw Martin as impertinent. He had a word with the local gardaí about this particular boy, who already had Martin in their sights by now. The gardaí knew exactly who had emptied the freezer.

*

Martin was adored by his parents and his mother idolised him. She was very proud of how he was always so polite with adults and he was forever helping her. The local women would tell Agnes what a lovely child he was, always good, always fixing things around the house and running errands for her. He always came up with little ingenious ways of making their lives easier. When the other children made carts to tear down the hill on, Martin was making it for a more useful purpose – for carrying coal and potatoes.

He was an extremely bright child whose cleverness and quick wittedness began to show at school. Rarely getting into trouble and headstrong to a fault, he displayed impressive powers of memory from an early age and could recall entire conversations from weeks previously. However, the master's strap was never far away. You could be on the receiving end of a severe beating for the simple crime of sneezing too loudly. If Martin came home with bruises, Agnes wasn't shy about marching up to the school and telling the offending master exactly what he was.

Martin began to get bored with school. Any attempt to do well was constantly put down by the masters, most of whom saw Martin as a brazen little know-it-all. They were much happier teaching 'thicks', as some of them called the children. A certain sort of satisfaction was achieved by leathering the bare bottoms of 'thick' little boys. They were never going to be educated; the masters at the school knew where these boys came from and knew where they were going – an education wasn't going to be needed. The teachers never trusted Martin because he could fly through the bit of work he was given. He'd do his sums and look up for more. They saw this as impertinence, so they would give him a few comics and send him to the back of the class for the rest of the day. Reading comics and pissing about in the classroom wasn't exactly stimulating. Martin began to miss the odd day. The teachers didn't give a shit anyway. So this was the way it was to be. Some of them were probably relieved – after all, he wasn't asking for any more sums. If he had banged his head off the wall and screamed for an education, they would have continued banging his head off the wall to knock any sense he had right out of him. He knew from a very early age what he was up against. It was only a matter of time before they ruined him. He knew he would have to rely on his wits to survive in this world.

He began to get into trouble. When he was just sixteen years old, he was brought before the Children's Court and given a two-year sentence for burglary. He was to serve this time in the industrial school in Daingean, County Offaly, which was controlled by the Oblates of Mary Immaculate order. He was delivered into the now notoriously known sadistic clutches of the order. Martin would go on to say, 'If anyone corrupted me, it was those mad monks in the bog.'

*

He held his breath as the cold grey van pulled up to the entrance of the industrial school for boys in Daingean. Daingean town is a miserable hole, just the right place for this towering monstrosity of filth, whose walls hid and bore witness to the child rapes and beatings savagely handed out by the monsters that were there to care for and educate the boys and show them the error of their ways. They showed them, all right. But Daingean was like a holiday camp compared to another industrial school where Martin's brother Eddie had been sent for school non-attendance – Letterfrack, a hell on earth.

Eddie was eventually transferred from Letterfrack, where he was flogged by the Brothers for running away from the institution. But Eddie was no pushover. There was no way he would take a beating lying down – he always fought back. They couldn't handle him in Letterfrack, so he was sent down to Daingean to join his brother, who by then had been there for a year.

Martin was completely different from Eddie – Martin turned away from confrontation, kept his head down and tried to do his time, whereas Eddie would run away from the place at any given opportunity. When the Brothers dragged him back, Martin would try to mediate, telling the Brothers that he would sort Eddie out, calm him down a bit. But Martin was proud of Eddie too. He saw the determination in his eyes and knew that Eddie had balls – no one was ever going to get the better of him. Eddie was always going to come out fighting. Martin's battles would not be fought alone.

Daily life at the school was hard. The bed was hard, the floor was hard, the walls were hard, the faces were hard, the fists were hard, the Brothers that ran the hellhole were hard. He would recall that the only warm thing about the place was the water, which came out from the taps boiling hot. All the boys had to wash in the wash room each morning, standing in rows in front of the line of brass taps that jutted out from the wall above a long communal sink, which ran down the length of the wall. 'Scrub those filthy ears, Cahill!' the Brother would shout. He blamed his pimples on the scalding water and he cringed as he put his red, raw hands into the water, as he knew the Brothers pissed into the sinks throughout the day. 'Come on, Cahill, scrub those pimples now,' a Brother sneered and waited for a reaction, but he never got one.

Martin never spoke to any of them. He kept his head down and watched them closely, and they knew it. They knew which boys to target, which boys were vulnerable. These were the ones that got the worst abuse, the ones that wet their beds night after night, the terrified ones, the tortured ones, the battered, spat on, pissed on, kicked, punched, buggered, torn to shreds, hair ripped out of heads, teeth pulled out, kicked out, kicked in, chests caved in, suffocated ones. But Martin was strong. He was big and muscular, exercising every day. He would jog for a couple of hours a day in the yard and use an old cartwheel as a weight, lifting it hundreds of times over his head. No one messed with him, but he was never a fighter. He was quiet, often helping the Brothers with their tasks and keeping the other boys quiet, stepping in and diffusing situations that arose. Some would say most of the Brothers were afraid of him. He rarely got hit by any of them. They gave him a bad haircut once, but that was about it. It was the boys on their own, the ones who had nobody, who suffered the most.

*

He could hear the faint groaning coming from the cellar. He nodded to his friend – it was time to move. The two boys crept down the winding staircase to the cellar that lay beneath the Brothers' quarters. Martin had sussed out this cellar months before and discovered it was an excellent little hideout. None of the Brothers came down here looking for boys, but for a couple of weeks he had observed one particular deviant who was well known in the institution for wanting more than the thrill of leathering children's bare bottoms with his belt. This man was extremely dangerous. Martin kept a close eye on him all the time. He had watched as the Brother took a thirteen-year-old boy called Patrick towards the cellar at least five times a week. He watched as he led the boy quietly, holding gently onto his shirt collar, smiling to himself as the boy lowered his head and closed his eyes. He knew what he was in for. Everyone did.

Martin crept down the stone steps, followed closely by another boy he trusted and had struck up a friendship with. The noise grew louder and louder the closer they came. Martin pointed to the sack and the shovel he had laid against the wall the previous night and his friend nodded in agreement. He knew what to do.

All of a sudden, they were behind the groaning pervert, who was on top of Patrick. Martin saw the boy's face, his features screwed up in a ball of pain, his eyes locked shut. Martin gave his mate the signal and they ambushed the Brother. Quickly covering his head and upper body with the potato sack, Martin picked up the shovel and brought it down with a crash on the Brother's head, knocking him out. He flopped to the ground, his upper body still covered by the brown sack. Martin pulled Patrick to his feet and covered Patrick's eyes with his hands. The boy was crying and his tears ran down Martin's hands.

'Run upstairs and keep running. Don't look back down here and don't look at us,' Martin whispered. Patrick nodded in agreement and fled as soon as Martin let him go, not once looking back. If the boy knew who had come to his rescue, the Brother would have beaten the information out of him. Martin tied the Brother's legs together with a rope he found on the dusty cellar floor and he and his friend made a quiet

exit back up to the yard and resumed whatever work
they had been given that day.

All hell broke loose that evening. The Brother who
had been raping the child that morning stood before
the congregation of defiant boys, each one looking at
this man with the contempt he deserved. Martin
watched as the Brother's face turned purple with rage
and he had to look away as white foamy drool slid
down the side of his chin. He went on a murderous
rant about how he would find the culprits that had
attacked him that morning as he was going about his
daily duties. When he found them, they would regret
ever having a thought in their heads, ever smelling,
ever seeing. They would be punished beyond anything
they had ever been punished for before. The Brother
pointed to his boots, huge black hobnails. 'The top of
my boot will be the last thing you will ever see,' he
warned. The boys stood silent, the only sound a tiny
sniff coming from the boy who had been raped that
morning.

That night, when the entire school was asleep,
Martin did something that would have been thought
of as next to impossible – he stole every single pair of
boots and shoes owned by the Brothers. He crept into
their rooms, into every closet, placing each shoe
carefully into his sack until he had cleared the place
of them all. He hid the sack in an old cart that lay in
the yard, covered with rubble, and waited for his
chance to get the sack of shoes out to the bog to bury.

Confusion and anger tore through the institution the next morning. The screaming and threats went on for the whole morning, but it was a mystery. Nobody knew, or was ever to know, what became of the shoes. Maybe in a thousand years bog excavators will dig up this mysterious bag of hobnail boots and wonder why they had been buried so long ago.

*

Martin left the industrial school a wiser person. He had witnessed firsthand what human beings are capable of and saw how people given power over others can abuse that power in many different ways. His character had been slightly hardened by his time at the institution, but they could not break his spirit, his true nature. It was going to take more than a gang of sadistic holier-than-thou scumbags to break him. Nothing he witnessed at that hellhole really got to him – he was strong enough to take it all in and not let it destroy him. It was just a chapter in his life, a time to get through in one piece, and his strength saved him, preparing him for the life that lay ahead. He decided that he would not allow himself to ever be in a position to be abused by those in authority again. He had to keep one step ahead of them at all times.

*

After his time in Daingean, Martin arrived back in Dublin, his home, where he belonged. He was eighteen years old and swore he'd never live outside the city. 'With the culchies? No way,' he'd laugh. While he'd been in Daingean, the family had been uprooted from their home in Crumlin by the Corporation in 1967 and given a three-room flat in a Corpo development in Rathmines called Hollyfield Buildings. He walked into Hollyfield with his sack over his shoulder. Groups of teenagers hung around on each corner, but they all stopped talking and stared as Martin strolled past, the girls giggling as he approached them. 'Any of youse know where the Cahills live?' he asked.

One girl squeezed through the tight group. 'Are you Mary Cahill's brother?' she asked. He smiled at her. The other girls started to laugh and pushed the girl forward and into his arms. 'Ah Fran, there's a lovely fella for ye,' they laughed and walked off.

Martin and Frances stood there gawping at each other. 'Well,' he asked shyly, 'where do they live?'

'Ah, yeah, just over there, number 10.' She pointed over towards the block.

'Thanks, Fran.' He smiled as he walked away, while she turned and ran laughing over to the gaggle of giggling girls.

*

He stood in the dark communal hallway looking at the group. The girls stood there nervously. One in particular, biting the corner of her lip, came forward. 'Yeah? Watcha want?'

Martin stood there leaning against the wall, his bottom lip covering his top lip. He looked at the girl and flicked a large silver dollar between his fingers, tossing it into the air and catching it. The girls watched the coin as if in a trance.

'Which one of youse wants to go to the pictures with me?' he asked, staring at Frances. The others knew that Frances was the one he was really talking to and she edged out to the front of the group.

'I'll go. What's the coin for? Is that real money?' He smiled and took her hand and they walked off together.

One of the girls shouted after them, 'Fran Lawless, he's no good, he's just out of borstel!' A hint of jealousy drifted along with the words.

Frances looked over her shoulder and smiled.

'Don't mind them,' he said. He looked at her and handed her the silver dollar. She thought he was loaded.

Martin started going steady with Frances Lawless shortly after they met on his arrival in Hollyfield. She was an attractive girl with large hazel eyes and hazel-coloured hair. She was very bright, the top of her class at school, and one of the very few girls that lived in the Buildings that actually took and passed her exams. Martin liked her quiet, easygoing manner. He couldn't abide women that nagged and he gave her no reason to nag him – she accepted him for what he was. She loved him.

When Frances got pregnant with her first child at
the age of fifteen, she and Martin got permission to be
married (supposedly, permission from the Pope
himself was needed for a fifteen-year-old to be married
– Martin was nineteen – but being in the family way
was permission in itself). They were married on a
frosty day in March 1968. The groom wore his best
suit and the bride wore a fashionable shift dress and
pillbox hat. Everyone in Hollyfield celebrated with the
young couple and they spent their wedding night in a
bed and breakfast down the end of Rathmines Road.
The next day at dawn, they rose to a sparkling
morning and Martin took his young wife by the hand
and walked around the city, watching the shopkeepers
getting ready for the day. He was happy – this was the
beginning of another chapter in his life. He was a
husband and soon to be a father. A tremendous feeling
of responsibility swept over him. He had everything
he loved. Frances was exactly what he needed, a good,
kind wife who would be with him through his journey.
He looked at his wife. She was really only a child –
they were both just a couple of kids – but they were
ready.

*

Martin and Frances lived at number 56 Hollyfield
Buildings. By the time she was twenty-one years of
age, Frances had three children. Their eldest boy,
Martin Jr., was soon followed by myself, a skinny, ugly

baby weighing only three pounds at birth and with not a blade of hair to be found on my body due to being two months premature. My father would always say they thought I was going to die, I was so small. Christopher was born three years later, in 1973. (Emma was born in 1980, just as we were leaving Hollyfield, and Luke came along in 1986.)

My mother and father were a happy young couple with plenty in common who rarely argued. They had very similar backgrounds, both having working-class parents. My mother's father was a 'gochie', a night watchman, who went out to work on his bicycle and returned at dawn. Both families were very dear to my parents and they were extremely close.

My parents never had a cross word against each other. Most of the time they were like a couple of teenagers, always sitting close to each other. He would lie on the sofa and she would rub his head. He was mad about her, always telling her how gorgeous she was and bringing her boxes of Cadbury Milk Tray chocolates.

Life was good; we were happy. Martin had everything he wanted.

He began working in the nearby Smurfit paper factory making cardboard boxes. He was a good time-keeper and got on with the job. His workmates would tell him to slow down, stop working so damn fast, he was making the rest of them look idle. He found the manager irritating after a while. One morning, when he was a few minutes late, the gaffer freaked. Martin was always early and this one morning had been the only time he'd been late. Martin knew it was only a matter of time before this fella's attitude became unbearable to him. He didn't like being told what to do. He was perfectly willing to do the work, but he was not prepared to take the 'I'm the boss' shit from some little manager with a God complex.

When one of the head fellas visited the factory one day on an inspection tour, he lost his wallet. Martin found the wallet and brought it to his manager the following day, not a penny missing. He was congratulated on his honesty. Little did they know, Martin had watched the wallet fall from the pocket onto the floor. He had kicked it under one of the machines to be retrieved later by himself, and the praise was his. He always kept his eyes open for small windows of opportunity like this.

The gardaí began following him home from work and it wasn't long before the factory boss was given the low-down on their model worker. They wanted to put a stop to his honest way of life – after all, if he wasn't out committing burglaries, they weren't going to get any medals. The job ended soon after that. Next stop, the dole.

*

I'm told my father began his housebreaking career from an early age. He had told me about robbing the priest's freezer, but this burglary business was something he never shared with his children. He would kiss us goodnight and leave with his gloves and torch. It was a regular ritual and we just got used to it. We didn't ask any questions and he never gave us anything to ask questions about. He was going out late at night even while he was holding down the job at the factory. Martin and his teenage brothers John, Eddie and Anthony, as well as Hughie Delaney, were out breaking into the big houses in the area, some nights breaking into between fifty and a hundred houses. More often than not, they left empty handed, their main objective being to cause havoc. The owners of these houses would be down in the Rathmines garda station the following day screaming that something had to be done about these thieves. It drove the police crazy. They would storm Hollyfield, beating anyone that crossed their paths. There were baton charges and arrests. They thought nothing of coming into your home and dragging you out in front of your family and laying into you with their batons.

The gardaí would stand in a line in riot gear at the entrance to Hollyfield and not let anybody in or out, but they couldn't keep Martin and his brothers locked in – they just went out the back way. There was nothing the police could do, really. Martin and his brothers and his brother-in-law, Hughie Delany, a close friend, would get out again and cause more mayhem, breaking into hundreds more houses. Again,

the police were on the receiving end of an angry and
frustrated public, and again heads would roll in
Hollyfield. When they got them into the station cell,
Martin's brothers would get unmerciful beatings, but
this was all part of the battle and they looked on their
injuries as war wounds.

They never beat Martin, though, and the beatings
his brothers got soon stopped when they hit their late
teens and the police began to realise that it only made
things worse – whenever anyone got a hiding, all hell
would break loose and they would go on a rampage.
Sometimes Eddie and Hughie would wander down
Rathmines pulling the hubcaps off cars and smashing
them through the windscreens. Each car on the road
would get this treatment and the trail of destruction
always led back to Hollyfield, just to let the police
know exactly who had carried out this particular act
of revenge against them. They had nothing against the
people who owned the cars, but it did give people a
small taste of what it was like to be on the receiving
end of harassment – and of course it drove the police
crazy. It was one big game of tit for tat. When the
police were free and easy with their batons, they
wanted these fellas in Hollyfield to just take it, roll
over and let them kick the shit out of them. It was
never going to happen. The gardaí were the enemy
now.

*

One of Martin's first enemies, before the family moved to Hollyfield, was the money collector, or as they called him, 'the Jewman'. Martin and his young brothers would watch him go from house to house collecting the shillings that each family owed him. They would watch as he left the houses and made little ticks in his notebook. 'The Jewman' was a regular caller to the Cahill household, as he was to everyone else in their neighbourhood in Crumlin. Martin had him in his sights.

He broke into the moneylender's house and went after his paperwork containing all the details of who owed what and when (there was never any money to be found, that was hidden far too well). The local gardaí in the station would try to pacify the moneylender by telling him that they would find the local gurriers that were doing this. Martin could see the anger in the faces of the police when they told him, 'We know it's you, you little bollox.'

By moving the family to Hollyfield, they were effectively pigeonholing Martin and his brothers. In the eyes of the police, the people of Hollyfield were unworthy of any sort of respect, condemned to a life of poverty. Who cared if the sewers ran out onto the footpaths? They classed the people who lived there as filth, and they were required to live in filth.

And it didn't stop when he was a teenager. It never stopped. The police were a constant presence his whole life, and in his family's lives. As Eddie Cahill said, 'Once you're branded a criminal, you have no voice, you're gone. The world is different to you then.'

Martin wasn't content to live his life trapped in poverty and he certainly wasn't prepared to bury his head in the sand and drink his way through the depression of living on buttons, like so many fathers did, or in his case hold onto a job that would eventually sap his energy and snuff out his flame. He was going out and doing what he knew, and he was good at it. He had made his decision and this was it, this was him, take him or leave him.

Chapter 2
The Buildings

Ireland in the 1970s was a time of rock 'n' roll, industrial strikes, hash smoking, barricades, parties, long-haired, peace-loving, police-hating people, long, hot summer days, petrol shortages and electricity blackouts. The rebellious nature of the decade was etched on the faces of the kids in those days – at least in our working-class corner of Dublin – and there was none more rebellious than Martin Cahill.

My father disliked the monotonous daily drudge that many people's lives were encased by. He liked things to be happening. He liked people speaking up for themselves, having a goddamn opinion. If you didn't like the way the government was treating you, speak up for yourself and do something about it. Don't sit back and whine about how you're being fucked by them – stand up to them and look them in the eye. Don't let them treat you like a tool to keep them in power.

For example, there was the time in the mid-1970s when lorries would rumble through the Buildings daily on their way to the factories at the back of the flats, even killing one child. This was extremely upsetting to all of us, so Martin organised a barricade. The trucks rammed these daily, only to be erected again the next day. He would not let us give up, and we didn't. Eventually the lorries stopped coming through our estate.

Martin was always backing people who had grievances with the system, and there was always some sort of protest going on in our lives. He was very interested in the trial and subsequent quashing of Peter Pringle's conviction by the Court of Criminal Appeal. We made 'Free Peter Pringle' posters and put them in our car windows. Dad made us take bundles of the posters into school with us and asked us to ask the teachers if they would display them in their car windows. We got some funny looks, that's all.

Peter Pringle was arrested on 19 July 1980 in connection with a raid on a bank in which a garda was shot dead. Peter was tried and convicted by the non-jury Special Criminal Court of capital murder and robbery and was refused leave to appeal. He served fourteen years and ten months. After the Criminal Procedure Act of 1993 was enacted, which allowed for him to appeal against his conviction, conflicting evidence by two garda witnesses at the original trial was brought before the appeal court as a newly discovered fact which rendered his conviction 'unsafe' and his conviction was quashed by the court. If the death penalty he originally received had been carried out, the 1993 Act would have come too late for Peter; thank God this isn't Texas. However, the court refused him a certificate which would enable him to claim compensation for a miscarriage of justice, and I believe his fight continues to this day.

A lot of IRA men on the run from the police would take refuge in the Buildings, with Martin putting someone up for the night more than once. They stood out to me because of their long hair and long beards and funny accent. At that time, the IRA was seen more as an organisation of petty criminals than a political army. By hiding these men, Martin wasn't helping the IRA per se, he was just sheltering someone on the run.

The only time there was any sign of trouble in our lives in those days was when the gardaí would drive through or the familiar dawn raids. Garda presence aside, our childhood was pleasant. There was always something happening – days were never dull, not with my father around.

*

Hollyfield was a glorious place for a child to grow up – well, in my eyes anyway – and as far as my father was concerned, there was no better place to raise a family. Hollyfield Buildings was our world. All of our family lived there: grandparents, aunts and uncles and friends from both my parents' side. Everyone knew each other and, like most flat complexes during the 1970s in Dublin, it teemed with children. We always had somebody watching out for us. There was always somebody you could trust to watch the kids or do you a favour or help you out in hard times. Family was everything to my father and he kept them close, no matter what.

My family was the largest family living in the Buildings. All my father's brothers lived there. There were always visitors to our flat. My father was always in the sitting room flanked by men: his friends, people he was being introduced to, people he was helping. He would sit in the middle of the group, speaking in a hushed tone, using his hands to gesture and explain. He was by no means a central figure, though – his brothers were very independent. No one told them what to do, not even Martin. If we kids got too noisy, we were ushered to the door and told to go out and play.

In Hollyfield, it was my father and mother and us three children – me and my brothers, Martin Jr. and Christopher. Martin Jr., the quiet one, always had his nose stuck in a book or making something with his modelling clay. Christopher was more like me, always out playing, climbing on anything and everything, and usually ending up in trouble or hurting himself. He was my father's pet and went everywhere with him.

I remember my father being quite strict when we were very young. He never allowed us to use bad language and he rarely swore himself. If we were being noisy or rude, he would let out a shout and we would soon stop. He never raised a hand to any one of us; I can't remember even so much as a little tap on the hand. My mother was much the same. There was lots of laughter and talking in our little flat. We also had four dogs and they were very much a part of the family.

We lived in a two-bedroom flat, which consisted of the two bedrooms, a living room and a scullery. There was a toilet, but there was no bath. We washed in a tub beside the fire. My father installed a shower when we got a bit older and there always seemed to be one relative or another waiting to use it, which wasn't surprising, considering it was the only one in the Buildings.

The occupants of Hollyfield Buildings were increasingly being segregated from the outside world, viewed as a mixture of outcasts, misfits, social lepers, thieves and scumbags. This was how the authorities wanted us to be branded, but it wasn't like that at all. Most evenings, friends would gather in our flat or in a friend's flat or sometimes everyone around a bonfire, listening to John Lennon blasting out over the loudspeakers that came from the windows of our flat. Most of the fellas would be gathered around my dad, laughing and joking and having a drink or a game of cards. (My father, though, didn't drink. He even had a Pioneer alcohol abstinence badge he wore on his collar. No one in Martin's circle drank very much; alcohol was never an issue. I never saw anyone getting drunk – it just wasn't the done thing then.) The women would chat amongst themselves until the party got started and then they would dance and sing. My father's brother-in-law, Eugene Scanlon, who was married to his sister Teresa, was a brilliant singer and musician who sounded just like Bob Dylan, and he would play the guitar and harmonica. It was a magical time of friends, family and togetherness. You can't match it today, in a world of neighbours who don't even know each other's names and most of today's children living their childhoods in crèches.

*

At the entrance to Hollyfield stood Tranquilla Catholic National School. Everyone in Hollyfield went there – well, at least until it was legal to leave. Martin Jr. and I went there up to first class. One night I was woken up by my father, who was lifting me out of bed. 'Da, what's wrong?' I asked.

'Come on down and see, the school is on fire.' He wrapped me in a big coat and carried me out into the night. The whole Buildings were cast in a glow of bright orange. The school was in flames. Everyone was out watching it, but I was upset.

'Da, all me drawings are in there, they're all burned now.' I began to cry.

'Ah no, they're not, everything good was taken out first. Don't worry, daughter,' he said and wrapped the coat tighter around me. I watched the flames through teary eyes.

The next day, we were told one of our uncles had

burned the school to the ground and we got our little drawings back, as well as a piano, which was brought into my grandmother's flat. My granny wasn't too pleased about the noisy thing, but she let us keep it.

*

Once I saw some young lad snatch a lady's handbag as she walked past the entrance to the Buildings. He grabbed her bag and disappeared into the flats. The distressed woman followed him for a short distance, but she soon turned and walked back out onto the road. She looked so helpless and upset. This bothered me greatly and when I told my father, he asked me who had grabbed the bag. He wasn't angry, but he was upset that I had witnessed this. The next day, hanging high up on the wall at the entrance to the flats was the women's bag, dangling by a nail.

My father didn't like us to be a part of things he felt to be inappropriate to our upbringing, and he would constantly remind us how important it was for us to go to school every day, never allowing us to miss days. I remember hiding under the bed if I stayed out of school and my father searching for me, shouting, 'Frances, come out! The school inspector will be after you!' I would eventually come out and put on my shoes. He would take me by the hand and walk me to school. 'You have to go to school. You won't learn anything by staying out,' he would warn me.

He helped with our homework and always

encouraged us to be enterprising. He encouraged any trace of talent in us and told us how great we were. No matter what it was, be it trumpets or ballet shoes, he got us what we wanted, even if the interest only lasted a week. He would say, 'If only I had a talent…it's a great thing.' When I passed my driving test at nineteen, it was as if I had won the Nobel Prize in his eyes. He was over the moon.

'Ah, Da, it's only a driving test,' I remember saying, but he wasn't having any of it.

'You did it yourself, daughter, no help. Fair play to ye,' he said. I think he was used to people giving the tester a bribe of some sort, which was common, but I didn't and he had enormous respect for that.

My father didn't spoil us as such. Family holidays were usually just a trip to the UK to visit relatives. He would never come with us, though; my mother would take us and he would stay in Dublin. 'I never go on holidays, but they always ask me to so they can have a holiday,' he once told reporters, referring to his surveillance team.

He would take us places in Dublin – the annual motor show in the RDS was a favourite, and a picture of the family with the car from the movie **Chitty Chittty Bang Bang** hung on the wall in our flat for years. He would take us to every circus that visited the capital. One time, at a visit to a circus that had a mother elephant with her cub, he became furious with the tamer, who continuously whipped the huge animal. He hopped over the barrier into the arena and took the whip from the startled tamer's grip. We looked on as he was led from the spotlight out to the back, behind the curtain. He came out a few minutes later, beaming from ear to ear. He took his ringside seat and the show resumed. That night, on our return home, our usual police escort followed close behind us. They stopped at the entrance to Hollyfield and watched us drive into the darkness – Dublin Corporation had switched off the street lights in our world long ago; we used torches to guide us to the entrance hall to our flat.

The next morning, I was woken up to the sound of my father's voice calling me from the street below our bedroom window. 'Frances, Martin, Chris! Wake up! Come on, ger up!' I didn't know what was happening. Martin and Chris got to the window before me and pulled back the hairy blanket which was put up to block out the draughts from the window. The sunlight flooded the room and I squeezed in between my brothers and stuck my head out through the window, which was missing a pane of glass. I screamed with delight.

Underneath our window, my da was sitting on top of the elephant from the circus. He had this huge smile on his face and shouted for us to come down. The fella from the circus also stood there, holding the animal by a rope which was tied to a huge collar that hung around the elephant's neck. We legged it down in our pyjamas, tripping over each other to get down first. We had a glorious day feeding the elephant and having rides around the pitch. My father paid the circus fella when they were leaving. It was a magical day for us kids, one I will always remember.

*

Martin told me once that sometimes when he came home at night, he'd sneak into the Buildings so the gardaí wouldn't spot him. He would sometimes go through a derelict building where a homeless tramp slept. Martin would quietly go past the snoring pile of rags that lay on the cold ground. One night, the tramp wasn't there and Martin went over to the pile of rags to see if he was okay. Underneath the pile he found an old tea can. He opened it and there was a watch, a wedding ring and a few pence, as well as a folded photograph of a smiling woman. He put the contents of the tin back, put a few bob into the tin and shoved it back where he'd found it. Anytime he passed the tramp after that, he'd shove some money into his tin for him. This had to be terribly confusing to the homeless person, but a welcomed mystery, I'm sure.

*

Martin rarely gave us pocket money, but most of his friends gave us a bit and his brothers spoiled us rotten. Martin always encouraged us to earn a few bob instead. At the back of Hollyfield, one of my father's old friends, Jemmy Byrne, kept horses in a stable and we would watch the horses being fed and groomed. I was sitting on the back of Da's Harley one day when he pointed to the horse shite on the ground. 'You see that, Frances? People put that on their gardens to help it grow.' The next day, my brother and I had it bagged and ready to be sold around the doors of the mansions that lined Palmerston Road. Other times, we gathered little bundles of sticks and sold them for firewood. My father would pat us on the heads and say, 'Fair play to ye, now you can get your sweets.' He was determined to make us see the value of money and also to be independent.

*

Our family stood out like a sore thumb amongst the other families in the Buildings, most of whom had nothing. We had a Mercedes Benz and a BMW. Martin's collection of motorbikes, which he loved, was growing – he had his Harley, Mother had a pink Kawasaki and we children each had our own child-sized motorbike.

But there was never any rivalry or jealously from the neighbours. Everyone knew that Martin had things and they could all come to him for money if they needed it. He rarely did any of his robberies for money. His goal wasn't to be rich – he never gave a damn about money or possessions. The fact he had these things drove the police mad. Amongst all the dirt and filth and sewage that ran through Hollyfield sat this big, gleaming, gold Harley Davidson.

Martin's passion for his beautiful, fast motorbikes was legendary. The day his Harley Davidson Electra Glide arrived in Hollyfield was a great day. The bike – probably the first in the country – cost him £7,000. He imported it through Germany and was a little angry when customs wouldn't allow collection of the bike without paying a further £7,000 in excise duty, but nothing was going to stop him having his Harley. He sent his mother down with the cash and then collected the bike. It was custom made, gold and white with gold revolvers attached to the boxes and a huge white leather saddle, with the Cahill family crest emblazoned on the back. He would take us out on it and we would squabble about whose turn it was next to ride pillion.

It was a wonderful thing. Everyone in Hollyfield loved it. He had speakers attached and his music would blast out as he rode along. Whenever he parked it in town, a crowd would gather around it. When he would return, he would watch the strangers from a short distance as they sat up on the bike, some even getting their photos taken on it. He would hang back and wait for the crowd to disperse; he was a little shy that way.

His collection of motorbikes grew to include a Yoshimara, followed by a Kawasaki, amongst others, mainly high-powered racing bikes, CBRs and Bimotas.

My mother soon learned to drive the motorcycles and he got her a pink Kawasaki. She would take us out for rides, but she was very cautious and drove slowly. We would shout at her through the helmet to speed up, but she wouldn't.

I had a small scrambler. I can remember Martin teaching me how to ride it: 'Pull the throttle slowly, slowly. Now take your foot off the clutch.' I shot off in the direction of a wall with him legging it after me. 'Pull the brake! Pull the brake!' he screamed after me.

But of course, the main reason he got his Harley was to spite the police.

Hollyfield was a shithole. The postman wouldn't even come into the Buildings, so the post for the tenants was delivered to the local shop. There was rubbish lying all over the place and rats ran up and down the walls. There were no drain pipes and sewage splashed up onto the Harley's wheels as Martin slowly pulled up outside our hall, but there the bike would sit, gleaming, amongst the dirt. It made the police sick. Martin would look out the window when the squad car or a little foursome of detectives would drive by, then slow down at his bike and look up. He'd wave and shout down to them, 'Ger up out of it, don't touch it!' They would slowly pull away, sneering at him. He loved it.

After a while, he rarely rode any of the bikes, but he would send us out with a bottle of polish and a rag to shine them up. But the bikes came in handy when

Martin and his brothers were trying to outrun the gardaí. Compared to what the gardaí were equipped with, it was like using a washing machine to chase a jet.

The kids would scatter when we heard the boom of a high-powered motorcycle tearing into Hollyfield, taking our places up on top of a wall to watch the drama unfold. My father, usually closely followed by one of his brothers, Eddie or Anthony, would drive up, park their motorbikes and disappear into the flats. We would wait, all eyes on the entrance to the flats. Twenty minutes would pass and a squad car would tear into Hollyfield and screech to a halt beside the bikes. Sometimes they would run red faced towards the halls that led to the inside of each block, but would give up when some dog would attack them, grabbing them by the ankles, and all the children would howl with laughter at this little show. It really was funny – the gardaí couldn't even outrun a mongrel dog, never mind catch my father on his motorbike.

*

'Where is he, Frances? Where is your husband?'

My mother sat in our small living room flanked by three detectives. I was woken by the familiar sound of a thick country accent.

'Wake up, you, come on.'

I rubbed my eyes and saw the strange face of a detective standing over my bed. My mother called for us children to come to her in the living room. I jumped out of bed and brushed past the detective standing in the doorway.

There were about seven detectives in our little flat, pulling out drawers and emptying out old biscuit tins that we used to keep letters and documents in. One of them asked me my name, and as usual I didn't answer. We were well used to these crack-of-dawn raids and knew what to do. My father was usually there, but this particular morning he was out.

'Where is that husband of yours, Frances? Now come on, Mrs Cahill, you know where he is.'

'I want a list of everything you're taking, and leave the children alone,' she replied.

We sat on the sofa as they tore the place apart. I watched blankly as they emptied my school bag out onto the floor. I was half hoping it was late and I would be too late to go to school, but I knew they always came too early for that.

During the many house raids we endured over the years, the whole family would usually be strip searched. We would be taken into separate rooms and told to strip naked. We were all well used to this treatment and were told by my father that we could not allow this to bother us – if we got embarrassed or showed any reluctance to strip, we were only giving the police satisfaction in the thought that we were humiliated by this treatment. I would strip off quickly, never waiting for the ban garda to tell me 'the knickers also'. I just took everything off and walked around the room and waited to be told to dress. When I was going through the awkward teenage years, though, it was quite hard not to be embarrassed, standing naked in my bedroom and being told to lift my hair, lift my arms, turn around, open your mouth by some ban garda, but I would stare her in the eye with a defiance my father taught us all to have from an early age. These people would not, could not, humiliate us.

My father would sometimes strip completely naked when he was stopped by a garda in his car on the street. He would walk up and down and the passing traffic would creep by, the occupants of the cars staring open mouthed at the spectacle. He didn't care, but it infuriated the gardaí – they were the ones with the red faces. They would tell him to cover up or be charged with indecent exposure. He would just laugh and get into his car and drive off in the nude. Once or twice I was in the back seat, cringing with embarrassment.

'Jaysus, Da, will you do that when I'm not in the car, for God's sake?' I'd say, laughing at him. He thought the looks on the guards' face was funny.

This time, though, my mother looked more worried than usual. I could sense there was something wrong in her voice. The police weren't worrying her; something else was.

The police left after an hour, with nothing but a few pieces of paper. They never did find what it was they were looking for, but they couldn't leave empty handed. As the last detective left, he said something strange to my mother. 'When you see Martin, tell him to keep out of the fields, he'll freeze to death,' he laughed as my mother closed the door after him.

That day, after returning home from school, my father was sitting on the sofa with my mother. We jumped up beside him and asked him where he'd been when the police were there that morning. He looked very dirty and tired and proceeded to tell us of the previous night's escapades.

'I was out walking when this car pulled up beside me. The police got out and dragged me into the car. They took me up into the mountains and tied me to a tree, but I escaped and ran down a big hill. The gang of police chased me, but I hid in the bushes and they couldn't find me,' he said with a smile. We sat there wide eyed, listening to his story. Years later, when I was much older, I learned how a number of members of the gardaí abducted my father that night, took him up to the Dublin Mountains and tortured him. He was to tell me later that if he hadn't escaped from them that night, he would have been found buried up in those hills.

Not long after this, by the late 1970s, a group of gardaí had become internationally notorious, even drawing attention from Amnesty International. This gang, labelled the 'Heavy Gang', which was formed by former Garda Commissioner Edward Garvey, who was replaced in 1978, was responsible for controversial investigations and wrongful prosecutions of Irish citizens. Writing in the **Sunday Independent** in 1989, Michael O'Higgins, SC, said, 'The gang were renowned for getting results. Suspects made confessions in custody which were often the only evidence against them. In court, the suspect would frequently attempt to retract his statement, which it was invariably alleged had been beaten out of him.'

This is what my father was up against.

*

A few months later, I witnessed the police abduct a child from the front of the flats. Myself and a gang of the local kids were out at the front of the Buildings, just playing around as kids do, when a blue car slammed on its brakes and stopped beside us. The door flung open and a huge detective jumped out. We all fled into the flats. As I ran, I turned around and saw the detective grab one of the little boys. I started to panic and turned back, screaming for him to let him go. He put the boy, who was hysterical by now, into the back seat, got into the car and sped off down the road. My heart was pounding as I ran to the boy's flat and screamed to his father, 'The police took John!' His father went inside and came back out with the biggest knife I had ever seen and headed off towards the police station. About an hour later, the boy was back out playing and looking rather brave and pleased with himself. That night, Martin told me how the boy's father had marched into the police station and past the desk without saying a word, picked up his boy and carried him home. They were lucky not to have opened their mouths; he would have surely used his knife.

The children in Hollyfield were all wise to the police. We knew that they could take out their baton and give it to you across the head if you got smart with them, and we knew that you should stay well away from one of the cells in the Rathmines garda station. We kept well away from them. But they would always pick us – Martin's kids – out of the bunch, singling us out. They would say to me, 'Your father's a thief, so watch where he puts his gun, won't you, and you come tell us where he's hidden it.' They would have a little laugh amongst themselves. I wasn't frightened of them and would march over and say something cheeky, like, 'Was there no room on the farm for you, ye thick? Keep away from us, you're all child molesters.' Now this, coming from a scruffy-faced little ten-year-old, would send them into a rage. We would just run away, laughing. My father taught us to answer them back, to never be afraid of them, but he also told us never to give them a reason to arrest you and to never be stupid. This is what they wanted to be able to do – brand all of us as troublemakers and thieves – but my father's battle with the law was personal and he wanted his children kept out of it.

We knew when the gardaí were driving through the flats – you would hear shouting outside and people would be hanging from their windows, yelling at them to get out. My da would rush from the window and out the door, laughing as we followed him up the landing to the railings on the top of the block to where we kept our little stash of rocks and glass bottles to hurl at the squad car. We kids used the rocks and my father used the bottles – he didn't want us to cut ourselves.

We had no fear that they would come chasing after us; they didn't have the nerve. They would drive quickly out of the Buildings to escape the hail of missiles coming from our childish hands and our laughter would echo down the hall as we returned home.

*

One evening, Martin heard that his brother Anthony had been taken into custody. He told my mother and Anthony's wife to go down and make sure that he was okay and that he had a solicitor down there with him. Martin stayed around the flat, looking after the children. When my mother returned, she looked very worried. They hadn't let them in to see Anthony and wouldn't co-operate with them at the desk, refusing to tell them whether or not they even had him. Martin put his coat on and left.

That night, we heard a loud commotion outside the door. When my mother opened the door, my father was carrying Anthony over his shoulder like a bag of coal. 'Get in, get in!' he shouted at us as he stumbled forward, his words echoing down the cold stone hall outside.

'Jesus Christ, Martin, what happened?' my mother asked.

'Shh, get him in on the sofa, quick,' Martin said.

Anthony was motionless when Martin lowered him carefully onto the couch. Thick, blackish blood covered his face, both of his eyes were swollen and purple and his lips were inflated, like balloons. He was frightening looking. My mother got a rag and some water in a bowl and gently tried to wipe the blood away. She and my father both kneeled over Anthony, who was still unconscious at this stage. Martin pushed his hair from his bloody forehead and quietly called his name. After a while, Anthony began to open his eyes.

When Anthony came to, his first words were, 'That bastard Ned Ryan.' The late Ned Ryan was one of the detectives who was part of the notorious Heavy Gang during the 1970s.

Martin had found him lying in a crumpled heap in a laneway behind the flats. At first, Martin walked past the figure, as it was quite dark and he looked like a heap of rags. But when he moved his torch over the figure, he saw his brother's barely recognisable face. He had been badly beaten and dumped in the laneway. The last person to see him was a friend of Martin's who was being released from a cell in the same police

station. He told Martin how he saw Anthony being
led into a cell, held by the arms.

Anthony's injuries were so extensive that the
doctor told his wife it looked as if he had been
trampled on by a bull. He had two broken arms, a
broken nose and fractured ribs. Ninety-eight per cent
of his body was black with bruising. His hair had been
pulled out in clumps and teeth were missing. Whoever
had done this to him had beaten and tortured him for
several hours.

Martin kept Anthony in our flat while he recovered
from his injuries. He didn't ask him anything about
what had happened and the children were given
instructions not to ask their uncle what had happened
to him. We would watch my father spoonfeeding his
brother and talking very quietly and gently to him.
After a few weeks, Anthony started to sit up and he
even managed a smile. We all knew then he would be
okay.

Anthony's revenge on Ryan for the attack was to
be in the form of poisoning. Martin didn't agree with
the plan but Anthony couldn't be told what to do.
Anthony trailed Ryan and watched his home for
weeks. He was going to insert a lethal substance into
the milk bottles that the milkman left outside Ryan's
door each morning. On the morning he planned his
revenge he decided against the idea when he saw a
child through the window. He wanted revenge on Ned
Ryan but he would never harm anyone else. Event-

ually, like everyone else, his bruises disappeared and he had his teeth repaired, but the grudge against the law grew deeper.

*

Our dislike of the guards initially came from my parents' warnings to us. My father would tell us stories of how they would beat people in the cells or plant things on you to put you away. We were warned never to speak to a policeman, not one word. If they spoke to you, you had to completely ignore them, pretend they didn't exist. We did this quite easily. He told us if we were ever arrested and put in a cell, we were to pick a point on the wall and stare at that point. We weren't to take our eyes off the point and had to think of something else. 'Block out their voices and don't listen to a word,' he'd say. Fortunately, we never had to put this into practice; we were never arrested. Except once.

My mother loved to take us to music festivals, and we always went to a popular festival in Lisdoonvarna in County Clare. We would arrive in our car and people would flock around us, thinking we were drug dealers just because Mother drove a Mercedes! On the way home from the festival in 1980, we were pulled over by the gardaí outside of Limerick, placed under arrest on suspicion of drug possession and taken to a local station. At the station, we were all strip searched, including my baby sister, who was about one year old, her nappy torn into little pieces. My brother Martin Jr. was taken to a cell and terrorised by gardaí, who told him that his family was gone and that he would be staying alone in the dark cell all night. They held him in a corner, standing very close to him at all times, calling him a little scumbag and telling him his father was a dirtbird. He was eleven years old.

We were released and left the station that same day. I think Martin Jr. was slightly shaken, because all the way home he just stared out the car window. But we never spoke a word to the gardaí in the station. We just stared at the floor, like Dad had taught us.

*

Martin spent four years in Mountjoy from 1975 to 1979 for possession of a stolen car – murderers get less time than that – and when he came out of prison, he found Hollyfield a different place.

Hollyfield had begun to fall into disrepair. The flats themselves were old and had no washing facilities (except for the shower that Martin had installed when we got too old to wash in the big tub next to the fire). The Corporation stopped collecting the rubbish and before long there were huge piles of it everywhere. Martin laid down pallets of wood at the entrance to the halls so we wouldn't have to wade through the sewage. I remember rats running up and down the walls, but I never remember anyone complaining.

Everyone knew that this was all a part of the battle. They wanted us to live in these conditions.

During the 1970s, no one seemed to care about the appalling conditions the residents of Hollyfield were enduring. But Mary Robinson, who was a well-known barrister at that time and later went on to become President of Ireland and the UN High Commissioner for Human Rights, came to see the deplorable conditions people were living in and told the residents to speak out against the government about it. Martin had huge respect for her. When no one else cared about the people in Hollyfield, she did. But my parents made the most of what we had. We loved the place; it was our home.

In 1978, Dublin Corporation began preparing to demolish the Buildings. Most of the families had moved out and my family and my mother's mother were the only ones left. My parents were appealing the eviction notice through the courts, a process my father had started while he was still in jail. Martin was determined to cause as much hassle to the authorities as possible. He wasn't leaving Hollyfield without a fight.

They began to knock the place down around us. I remember sitting on the floor of our flat, frightened, the whole building shaking as the demolition ball pounded the walls. Then they turned off the electricity supply to the flats. My mother would burn an old antique oil lamp in the room. As children, we found this quite exciting, but it must have been unnerving for my mother. Martin would read us bedtime stories under the light of the oil lamp. He managed to reconnect the electricity, but the Electricity Supply Board quickly turned it back off. He reconnected it again and they ripped up the underground cables to prevent him from reconnecting. He put on some yellow reflective rain gear and some thick rubber gloves, got down in the hole where the cables were and reconnected the electricity supply yet again. Every time the light came back on, we would let out shouts of joy and quickly turn on the television. He would walk through the door as if coming home from his job, beaming at us as we thanked him.

The place began to pile up with muck and rubble. The kids thought it was a great place for playing, but when my brother Christopher was bitten by a rat and was in danger of having his foot amputated, my mother couldn't stand it any more. She was offered a three-storey house in Kevin Street, in the heart of the Dublin Liberties. She took it.

But Da hung on in the Buildings. After losing the appeal for the eviction, he closed the door on number 15 and on a part of his life. But he still didn't give in – he put up a caravan on the building site that was Hollyfield, just to annoy them. His little caravan was taken away, but even that didn't stop him – he put up a tent. When the tent was burned, he reluctantly came down to join us in Kevin Street, right across the road from a garda station. Great.

Chapter 3
No One Wants to Talk About Robberies Any More

After Hollyfield Buildings was demolished in 1980, we moved into a Corporation house in Kevin Street. This estate of red brick houses in the Liberties area of Dublin stood directly facing the Kevin Street garda station. My father suspected this was a deliberate attempt by the police to try to humiliate him. He hated the house but didn't mind the area, but we all missed living in Rathmines and it took a while for him to get used to not being in Hollyfield. He felt we didn't belong in the inner city, so he decided we would eventually move back to Rathmines – and he usually got what he wanted in the long run.

My father had a lot of respect for the people who lived in the area. During the 1980s, the drug problem in these areas was starting to devastate the lives of many young people and their families, and my father detested the people who profited from this misery. He was a firm supporter of the concerned parents' groups that began to form, people who were forced to take to the streets to try to protect their children from heroin. These people had been let down by the government and he fully understood their frustration and desperation.

However, like most things, corruption set in and the parents' groups turned into vigilantes that began to patrol the streets, some of which were drug dealers themselves, using this as a cover-up to carry on their wicked trade. Martin had no time for hypocrites. He said it was only a matter of time before petty burglars, most of whom were drug addicts, became the target of these vigilante groups, who painted everyone from handbag snatchers to drug pushers with the same brush. He wasn't wrong. Punishment beatings were regularly carried out and no distinctions were made between known criminals who had nothing to do with drugs and the dealers.

These vigilante groups became above the law, with the full backing of the police, who would cordon off the area and watch from the sidelines as these groups would march up to a house and throw the whole family out, furniture and all.

Martin's friend Shavo Hogan was targeted. They only started going after these fellas with convictions because they were told to by the police. Martin backed the concerned parents' groups, but didn't believe in vigilantes.

Martin had to deal with the scourge of drugs within his own family – two of his younger brothers became addicted to heroin and he did everything he could to help them, even going so far as to lock one brother in a room for a month to detox, feeding him and talking to him for hours on end. We would hear his screams of pain as he went through withdrawal cold turkey, but my father explained that this was a normal part of the detox and was necessary to try to save our uncle's life. And his life was saved, but months after his detox he was back on the drug again. Martin went on to say that trying to rescue a person from heroin was like pissing against the wind. The only thing that could save them was themselves; they had to want to be saved. Drugs were a huge sadness in my father's life. He would say how times had changed: 'No one wants to talk about robberies any more, it's all drug talk.'

Hughie Delaney, Martin's brother-in-law and trusted friend, also fell victim to drugs and died from an overdose in the early 1980s. His death was a huge blow to Martin. During this time, Hughie's wife, Una, Martin's younger sister, a beautiful dark-haired girl the image of her mother, had also succumbed to drugs and had received a long prison term for possession, leaving their seven-year-old son on his own. What's more, Una became mentally unstable in Mountjoy, eventually being sent to the Central Mental Hospital at Dundrum. They were just two more reasons for Martin to despise the misery of drug addiction.

*

The drug problem in Kevin Street began to get out of hand. Everyone knew the local drug-dealing family, headed up by a rotund, middle-aged matriarch whose sons dealt in the local supply. Martin knew a couple of the brothers, but he never had any time for them. He did see that a certain member of this family was a danger to children, in more ways than one, and he warned one of the local mothers that her young teenage son was in the control of a dangerous, manipulative child molester who was using the local boys to run around for him. The mother was obviously shocked and frightened, but she believed Martin when he said she had to do everything in her power to keep her son away from this deviant.

If Martin saw something wrong going on, he would never sit back and allow it to continue. He absolutely loathed the drug scene and all the rotten heartache that trailed behind it. The man that was using and abusing the children was given an ultimatum to stop what he was doing to the local kids or he would be hung from a lamppost. When we eventually moved from the area in 1983, the drug dealing continued. When the teenage boy in question was found dead one morning, the blood drained from my father's face when I told him what had come of him. He hung his head and said, 'What a waste. What a bloody waste.'

*

Martin's brother Anthony was only thirty years old when he died from an apparent drugs overdose in March 1983 while serving time at the Curragh military prison.

The Curragh was as tough a prison as they come. The Curragh Camp housed an overflow of prisoners from Portlaoise Prison. It wasn't like a normal prison – some of the cells were even padded. When you did your time down there, the time was hard. Prisoners protested about numerous human rights violations. If there was ever a prison that could break a spirit, it was the Curragh, which during the 1970s was also used to detain political prisoners. Anthony was cut from the same cloth as his brothers and he stood up to the regime, but it was a regime designed to break you.

For instance, during a prisoner protest at the Curragh Camp in March 1980, Anthony was assaulted by military policemen in riot gear. When he refused to submit to an internal body search, he was beaten half to death, after which a high-powered hose was turned on him and he was left in the wet clothes and confined to his cell for days. Anthony would have never asked for help from anyone, especially the courts, but Martin was on the outside and said, 'Fuck this, take it to court.' He applied to the High Court for an enquiry pursuant of Article 40.4.2 of the Constitution into the legality of Anthony's detention. He also claimed that the prison was in breach of the Prison Act 1972 (Military Custody) Regulations.

No one really wanted to go to the courts. Eddie said that they didn't want to appear to be whinging, as this just gave the screws an excuse to taunt you, and anyway, everyone knew that the courts would rarely find that a constitutional right had been breached. But Martin brought the enquiry to the High Court just to see what would happen.

During the enquiry, the court found the prison's breaches of regulations to be unacceptable and recommended that the confinement of prisoners to cells to effectuate loss of privileges should stop. The court also found that the lack of education programmes at the prison was totally unacceptable – after the enquiry, books were to be supplied to the prisoners. However, the court did not find any breaches of constitutional rights. It found any physical restraint used was justifiable. This particular prisoner wasn't going to get his rights back. This came as no surprise to Martin. The Department of Justice eventually took over the military detention centre in 1998 and now uses it as a civilian prison, but that all came far too late for Anthony.

Anthony was beginning to crack. Nobody wants to do their time the way he did, being constantly picked on, poked at and harassed by the screws. Anthony's motto mirrored Eddie's: 'You either kill me or leave me alone.' Anthony, however, was not left alone. It was a nightmare.

Anthony found something that would help make the time pass a little easier – drugs.

Martin didn't know that Anthony had turned to drugs at the prison. When he and Eddie got word from Anthony that he needed to get out of this place, now, they discussed it amongst themselves and weighed up the options. Anthony wanted them to ambush the prison van that brought prisoners to and from the court and other places, but the Curragh Camp was run by armed soldiers. Martin and Eddie decided that since Anthony had so little time left to do (about ten months out of a five-year sentence), it was no harm for him to serve the rest. Anthony died in the prison six months later. Eddie believes it was more than a simple overdose, that Anthony killed himself because he couldn't cope any more.

Anthony's death broke my father's heart. He lost both of his parents in the same year as Anthony, all three just months apart. Martin put his mind to other things and got on with it, saying, 'Never regret anything. You can't turn back time. There's no use thinking what if.' He had a tough exterior, but a part of him went with Anthony.

*

I remember Martin telling us as children, 'Stand up to them. Never show them fear. They will try to make you afraid. Be careful!' He trusted our judgment and let us make up our own minds. Even as children, we saw what the gardaí were doing. We saw the wrong, the hurt.

With my own eyes I saw the bruises my teenage friend endured at the hands of gardaí. In our old photographs, we are carefree girls, hugging and pulling faces – far from the photographs she hesitatingly showed me one night of her black eyes, hair standing on end and a face so swollen her own mother couldn't recognise her.

She was a nineteen-year-old girl standing on the corner with her boyfriend. The gardaí arrived and were irritated by them standing there for no apparent reason. They told them to move. My friend and her boyfriend giggled and they heard the crackle of a police radio. She remembered little more of that night.

The gardaí on the beat had called for back-up. And back-up came, in the form of ten to fifteen gardaí in a black van. My friend was set upon by them like a pack of wolves on a fox. They kicked her until her eyes closed and stomped on her so hard she blacked out. She was just a girl, a girl in the back of a police van being kicked and stomped to shreds. She remembered waking up in the blacked-out cell, and looking out of her eyes that could hardly open, she saw the gap in the door. Surely there was someone there on the other side that could help? She put her hands over her eyes and prayed for it to end. It didn't. They came in again and beat her with batons. She didn't feel a thing; all feeling was gone now. Her father collected his desperate daughter from the station the next day.

When I showed my father the photographs of my friend's beaten face, he wasn't shocked like I was. He just looked at me and said, 'You know, this happens all the time in police cells across the country. Learn from it.'

My friend took a court action against the gardaí for this treatment and won compensation in an unreported Circuit Court case.

We never feared the gardaí. Martin instilled an aloofness in us towards them. Once you're not afraid, you're free.

*

Shortly after we moved to Kevin Street, the garda harassment and intimidation grew. They were a constant presence in our lives, following Martin closer than ever, so whenever he left the house and the gardaí weren't to be seen, Martin's suspicions would grow.

One morning, when Martin went to his car, which sat outside our back gate, his suspicions began to rise as, oddly, there were no gardaí about. He looked through the windows of the car, but saw nothing unusual. He opened the boot and searched it, smiling when he found the gun, a Colt .45 wrapped in black tape. He didn't touch it, but quickly called his solicitor's office and told him that he had discovered a gun in the boot of his car and that he believed a member of An Garda Síochána had planted it there to frame him. His solicitor told him to leave it there and he would inform the guards of the find.

That afternoon, detectives from a nearby station called to Martin and asked him where the firearm was. He began hurling abuse at them, telling them they knew exactly where the fucking thing was because they had probably planted it there themselves. The detectives took the gun away and that was the last Martin heard of it.

After that, he began to stick Sellotape in various positions on the car boot and doors. He knew that if the tape was disturbed, then more than likely someone had tampered with his car and may have planted something there. He had to have his wits about him at all times.

It was also during our time at Kevin Street that Martin began to wear his trademark balaclava mask or cover his face with his hand any time he went out in public so that the gardaí wouldn't be able to pick him out in a line-up. If you look closely at photographs of him in his ski mask, you'll often see that they're turned inside out. He told us that this was because the seam running down the middle would wear a line into his forehead, so by turning it inside out, it wouldn't annoy him so much.

*

We never did settle into life in Kevin Street very well. Martin was worried about the ever-growing drug problem and was afraid his children would fall victim to the scourge that threatened to wipe out the teenage years of many of the vulnerable kids in the area. However, the neighbours in Kevin Street were good down-to-earth types who accepted us into the community. My mother and father would drive into the estate on their motorbikes, she on her pink Kawasaki and he on his Harley or one of his racing bikes. Needless to say, they were quite different from my friends' parents.

It was during our time at Kevin Street that the police harassment and attempts to frame him rose to fever pitch. Martin had a posse of detectives following closely behind him most days. Unlike living in Hollyfield, where we were the only witnesses to the bizarre goings-on in my father's life, the neighbours and the kids were curious to know why Martin always covered his face with his hand when he came out of the house and why he was always followed by groups of men, most of whom were dressed in shirts and ties. Very strange altogether. My reaction was to simply tell the truth. I was only a kid at the time.

'Ah, that's nothing. They're the police and they follow my da around all the time. They're trying to frame him, so he covers his face so he won't be stitched up by them on a line-up.'

My new friends just gawped at me, wide eyed. I could have been speaking Swahili for all the difference it made – they couldn't understand and rarely mentioned it again. In time, though, neighbours eventually got to know us and then my father had a whole new batch of people coming to him for various reasons. To some, he was the one you could turn to when you desperately needed help. He gave people money – money for new windows, money for a business idea, money to pay off loan sharks. One thing I do know: he rarely got any of this money back and he never went looking for it. He was happy for people not to forget and maybe they could do him a favour in return one day.

Chapter 4
Ready for Round Two

We were glad to move to Cowper Downs in 1983. My father was back where he was happiest – Rathmines.

However, the new house in Cowper Downs still needed a lot of work. Martin went on to have an argument with one of the builders in the estate – my father believed that this person was passing on information to the police about who was buying the Cowper Downs house. The unfinished row of houses in the estate was set alight one night, causing extensive damage to the roofs. Martin wouldn't let anyone think that they could cross him.

But a snag list was the last thing on Martin's mind – he couldn't wait to move in and start building his pigeon lofts.

Martin started his hobby of keeping pigeons from the age of ten, when he would spend his afternoons cleaning out his small, ramshackle loft and sit on the roof, whistling loudly, overjoyed as his plump birds landed on him, covering his head and outstretched arms. He told me that racing his pigeons brought him back to his childhood and the immense enjoyment he got from looking after his birds. When deciding to buy a place in Rathmines, he cared more about the site's situation and the size of the garden than the house itself. The house was merely a secondary consideration. Number 17 had the largest garden and it had a good aspect for spotting approaching racing pigeons coming in from France and England.

We paid £80,000 for the property, which was quite a lot in those days. We never cared to think where the money had come from to buy the house, but he told us his mother had left behind a lot of money when she died and that most of the money was borrowed or owed to him from business friends.

The only thing wrong with Rathmines was the garda station; otherwise it would have been a perfect place to live. The Rathmines station was dirty and dingy and stood out as an eyesore on the street. However, Rathmines was great for promotion in the ranks and most of the gardaí assigned to the station were ruthless and ambitious. The detectives that were to question Martin never laid a hand on him – they were too frightened of what he would do outside of the cell, when they were alone in the dark. His reputation as someone who could appear in your room at night frightened the life out of them. But their tough reputation was no joke to those who ended up on the receiving end of garda interrogation.

*

When we lived in Cowper Downs, a local family's mother would beat her children and lock them in a playhouse they had at the end of the garden. We would hear the children wailing and then whimpering at night in the playhouse. One time, when I was around fifteen, I could hear her beating one of the children and I looked over the wall to see what was going on. The mother was lashing the boy – he must have been about eight years old – across the back with a pole in her side lane. She was practically frothing at the mouth, until she saw me staring at her.

That night, my father got into their house and decided to have a look around. I had given him all the gory details of the boy's beating earlier that day, but it wasn't news to him. My parents had reported this local child abuser to the social services on many occasions, but it went nowhere (the lesson to be learned was that if you have money in Ireland, you can get away with just about anything). Anyway, everyone was in bed. He looked in on the parents – she was happily reading in bed, her hair in curlers, while the husband snored contently. The kids' rooms were locked. When he unlocked the doors, he discovered the children tied to their beds, fast asleep. He could do nothing but leave. And so began a new day in middle-class Ireland, where Martin Cahill was the bad guy.

He made another report to the social services, but nothing ever happened and no one from social services ever got back to Martin about his report. He confronted her in the street one day and roared at her about the abuse her children were suffering. There was a for sale sign up on her house the following day.

*

Martin loved animals and we kept many dogs. In Hollyfield we had four purebreds: a huge Bull mastiff called Max, a Doberman called Prince and two Kerry Blues, Caesar and Gary. He loved the dogs and he always fed them sheep heads, boiling the heads in a huge pot on the hob. It was a little scary to look at and I would run past the cooker. A fella he called 'Sheep Head' would deliver the heads to him each week; they must have come from a slaughterhouse somewhere. Later he had another large dog, also called Max, a Rottweiler with a vicious temper. While we lived in Kevin Street, the police would torment the dog by sitting on the garden wall and hitting him with sticks from above. It turned him into an excellent guard dog, and God help any one of them that fell in on top of him. Later on, when we moved into Cowper Downs, the Rottweiler came with us. The police continued to torment the animal and he was so vicious nobody but my father could control him. The dog only feared him; everyone else wilted if the dog came close.

One day, I heard a huge commotion outside. I could hear car horns hooting outside and a lot of voices crisscrossing over each other. Da was home.

There was an unusual amount of noise, so I left my desk and went to the window. A smile crept slowly over my face. My father had arrived at the house followed by his usual entourage of police escorts. He had a few of his very close friends with him too, so all in all about four cars pulled up outside the gate. Now all of these cars also had their escorts, so at least ten or eleven cars were outside the house now. My father was walking slowly into the house, followed closely by his friends. My father had his familiar anorak on and his hood over his face, which he'd been wearing since the early 1980s; he found it less tiring to wear the hood now instead of having to cover his face with his hands all the time. They were all laughing and my father's friends shouted insults back to the police, who at this stage were hanging from their car windows and standing on neighbours' walls shouting abuse at my father, like, 'Martin, you fat bastard, we'll get you, you baldy fat cunt!' My father laughed and waved and his friends shouted back at them.

I came down the stairs and my father went into the living room, pulling his hood off and ruffling his hair back in place. His friends followed. They all sat down and Da called for me. 'Any chance of a drop of tea, Frances?' He gave me a glance and a little smile that said please.

I brought in the tea on a big tray and all of them reached forward and took their tea, still talking and laughing with my father as they dunked their biscuits into the cups of steaming tea.

'Thanks, daughter,' my dad said as I left the room. On the way out the door, I caught a glimpse of two detectives standing on our wall, trying to look in the window. 'Da, would you look at this?' I said. He stood up and went to the window, laughing as he pulled the curtains.

I went into the back garden and let Max out the side gate, intending to take him for a walk. Now this dog, a ferocious-looking Rottweiler, was a pet, but with the police standing on the wall and towering over him day after day in a threatening manner, the dog's attack instincts took over. As we passed the two blokes – youngish dicks, they didn't look very experienced – the dog dived onto the detective's leg. The other detective legged it. I held the dog by his thick studded collar and shouted at him to stop, but he wasn't letting go, not for anyone. The detective was slapping Max on the face and squealing for me to get him off. I couldn't. I yelled for my father to come.

The dick was getting frantic at this stage. As he wildly hit the dog repeatedly on the nose, the dog's grip grew tighter and his growling intensified. Although the animal only had him by the trouser leg, the detective was becoming delirious – the dog's mouth wasn't the only one foaming. My father came out through the front door with his hood over his face. Seeing this, the detective pulled out his firearm. As my father approached us, more detectives gathered around the scene. 'I'll shoot him, I'll fucking shoot him!' the detective shouted, pointing the gun at the dog's head. I frantically pulled at Max's collar.

'Frances, get in the house,' my father said. I let the dog go and Max swung around, pulling the detective to the ground. With this, the other detectives lurched forward. A couple of them took out their guns and pointed them at the dog. My father moved in. 'Max! Come here!' Everyone fell silent as the dog released his grip and ran over to my father. He followed him into the hall, panting loudly with a big steamy smile on his excited face. I watched as the detective left the garden, shaking, and returned his gun to its holster. The next-door neighbour was standing there, mouth wide open, her gaze following the police as they got back into their cars, a look of disbelief on her face.

In 1988, Martin was sent to Spike Island prison in Cobh, County Cork for a brief spell for contempt of court, during which time Max died. He was like a puppy at the end, his body riddled with cancer. He died on our dining room floor after we took turns spoonfeeding him drops of water. We buried him in the back garden.

A couple of weeks later, we were woken up by the familiar banging on the front door, another police raid. (The law never ring doorbells.) They searched the house – we never knew for what – then moved on to the garden and began to dig up the back. I was looking out of the upstairs bedroom window when I noticed that they had come across the area where the dog was buried. When we had buried the dog, we put an old door over the body, then covered it in with soil. The police banged down hard on the door with their shovels and began to look excited, thinking they had come across a bunker of some sort, Martin's buried treasure. When they lifted the door and discovered the rotting corpse of the dog, they jumped out of the hole, cringing. One of them called for a couple of rookies to come and lift the dog out of the hole to check underneath it. Nothing. They left that day, leaving the dog exposed on the half dug-up lawn. We buried him again when they left. Was it a Vermeer or a Goya they were hoping to uncover? Or perhaps a stash of guns? We can only wonder.

*

One night shortly after his return home from the prison in Spike Island, he came in the back door of the house covered in dirt, police cars screeching outside. They knew he had been on the loose and they had lost him. He looked a little shaken.

'Quick, Frances, get me my torch and another jacket upstairs.' I quickly did as I was told and he then told me to turn out all the lights in the house. Everyone else was in bed, so the house was very quiet. 'Get your coat on, something dark, quick!'

I pulled on a jacket and whispered, 'What's wrong, Da? What's wrong?'

'Shush,' he said, putting his finger to his lips. 'Come on.'

We went out to the garden. It was very dark and there were no police on the wall yet. He quickly scrambled over to the fence, removed part of the panel and went through into the garden next door. I followed and he put the panel back. We crouched down in the grass and got to the other fence, which we climbed over, and then another and another until we were out on the main road and walking down the footpath to a car he had waiting. I was very tired after that. I wasn't used to clambering over fences, but my father hardly broke a sweat. He drove a short distance up around Dodder Park and we left the car. We walked a short distance, then came to a building site where a couple of diggers were resting on mounds of soil.

'I buried something here, daughter,' he said. 'I came up to get it, and look what's happened.'

I began to smile and bit my lip. 'You're messin', Da.'

'No, I swear,' he smiled. 'I buried some money here and now look, these bastards are after diggin' it up. It's probably in a landfill somewhere.' He began to laugh. I couldn't hold in my laughter any longer and we both went into hysterics.

'How much was it?' I squealed, trying to contain the noise.

''Bout one hundred grand.' He put his hand to his mouth to stop laughing.

I pressed my lips together hard and swallowed. I laughed so hard that tears fell onto my cheeks and I brushed them away. We stood in silence for a while in the darkness, looking at the uprooted earth.

'Ah well, fuck it, it's only money. It's gone now, good luck to whoever finds it.'

We turned and walked away and he never mentioned it again.

*

One of my father's passions in life was his racing pigeons. It was his hobby, something to take his mind off things. He loved everything about the sport. Pigeon racing was old, working-class Dublin, and it brought him back to the nostalgia of his childhood. He owned hundreds of stock and racing birds. The garden in Cowper Downs was filled with spotlessly clean pigeon lofts and aviaries that housed his prize-winning birds.

All week long, he'd spend his time cleaning the lofts and training his pigeons. He wore an anorak stained with bird shit and he would emerge from the loft with his dust mask covering his mouth and feathers in his hair. Saturdays were race days. He and my brother Christopher would sit staring at the sky for hours, tin can in hand. The can held corn, and when it was shaken the pigeons would rush towards the loft. Martin would jump up as soon as he saw the bird in the distance. 'Quick, get the clock!' he'd yell.

He and Chris would run into the loft and furiously shake the can filled with corn. The birds would home into the loft and win him another trophy.

Throughout all of this, the gardaí would just sit on the wall, staring at them. They never frightened the birds away – I think they knew never to cross that particular line. They would just open the traps and let a cat in at night instead.

He was always happy pottering about in the lofts and constantly had visitors to the loft, men from the Dublin pigeon racing community. The gardaí would be up the road stopping everyone that was heading for our house – you had better hope your car tax was up to date – but Martin loved the way all of the fellas from the pigeon club never mentioned the gardaí harassing them outside on their way up to see him. They had more important things to talk about – pigeons.

The men from the club would walk from loft to loft, following my father, admiring his birds and hoping to leave with a youngster that would some day win them one of the cups Martin had in his dining room. His birds won him and my brother Christopher – another dedicated pigeon man – hundreds of prizes, from cups to trophies, certificates and prize money. (Martin gave any money he won back to the club.)

He had real friends in the pigeon club he belonged to down in Ringsend. All its members knew and respected Martin. I still remember the wreath they sent to the graveside when he died. It said: 'Martin, thank you, from everyone at The Premier RPC, Pearse Street.' It meant a lot to us.

*

Life in Cowper Downs was strange. One thing I will say is that by and large, the neighbours were okay. Everyone wants privacy, and these people were no different in that regard. They were tolerant in a half-smiling sort of way, and in some outlandish way we belonged, or were at least respected. My father didn't want to make life difficult for our neighbours.

Behind the lofts at the bottom of the garden was the neighbour's wall. A well-known builder named Sisk lived over this wall, in a house surrounded by an immaculate garden that housed perfectly pruned rose bushes and impeccable lawns that were seldom walked upon. Sometimes I would watch the elderly couple potter about in the garden, checking that their gardener had done a good job on the flowerbeds. The only blight on Mr Sisk's landscape was the Special Branch car that nestled on his driveway and the sound of a police radio contaminated the gentle babbling sound that came from his fish pond.

Martin had absolutely nothing against the Sisk family – that is, until they started to allow the Special Branch detectives to access their property for the sole purpose of intimidating and harassing my family. Mr Sisk was letting the gardaí use his property for access onto his wall, where they could watch our family and hurl abuse and rubbish at us as soon as we stepped out into the back garden. The police would sit drinking beer on the wall and throw the cans at my teenage brother as he went about looking after the pigeons. They would spit at my mother and call her a prostitute as she hung out the washing. Their high-powered search beams would shine through our bedroom windows all night long. Without Mr Sisk's co-operation, none of this harassment would have been possible.

It wasn't exactly a neighbourly thing to do. After all, my father had never done anything to the Sisks for them to have a grievance towards our family. Maybe they didn't like the pigeons. But my father didn't really blame them. He knew that they were being used by the gardaí and he felt rather sorry for them.

So it came to be that a group of detectives put together by the big wigs in the police headquarters in Phoenix Park to watch my father's every move, every second of the day, seven days a week, perched on this wall at the back of our garden.

Martin would bring them out cups of tea on cold days and they would just kick the cups off the wall and spit out venomously, as if he had offered them poison. My father would come laughing into the kitchen, saying, 'Betcha he was dying for a cup of tea.'

The detectives, most of them new to the post, must have been excited when they were briefed on their assignment. They must have been sure that their days of boring cases and reporting were at an end. How disappointed they looked, sitting forlornly on that cold wall, watching Martin Cahill scrub pigeon shit off the floors of his loft. Surely this man – this crime boss, this arch villain – was going to give them excitement, juicy stories to discuss with the wife in bed at the end of a hard day's watching. Sadly, no. 'I'm a bore. It's boring, surveillance. Take it from me, they're bored,' Martin once told a reporter.

Or at least, not all of the time. My father began to feel a bit sorry for them, sitting there all day with nothing to do, so he began to entertain them.

One day, while listening to his records in the kitchen, he had an idea, something to perk up the dreary neighbourhood. He got a loudspeaker and climbed to the roof of the loft. The surveillance guys hopped from the wall and the others that were snoozing in the dick car stirred to life.

'Mr Sisk, come on out, Mr Sisk, I'm gonna sing you a tune. Do you like Frank Sinatra, Mr Sisk?'

The detectives started to shout at him. 'Get fucking down, Martin, we'll do you for breach of the peace!'

Dad continued with his little show. He began tap dancing up and down the length of the loft, singing and clicking, making tap dancing sounds. The detectives stared at him through their brand new balaclavas, fuming. One even threw a rock at him, but missed. 'Ah, I'm not that bad, am I?' Martin said.

He then turned his attention to another neighbour, ex-Taoiseach Garret FitzGerald, who once claimed that Martin's pigeons had eaten up all the grass seed in his freshly made lawn. Here the banter got slightly more obscene. 'Mr FitzGerald, does your wife give these fuckers blow jobs as well as you, you fucker? Come on out to the garden. Wheel the wife over and she can do the country a service. Come on out, Mr FitzGerald. Mr FitzGerald, come out, Mr FitzGerald,' he bellowed over the speaker. The detectives were shouting at him to give it up, but he was on a roll. He eventually got down and walked slowly towards the house. I was in the kitchen. He came in and pulled off his mask. I started laughing with him and all I said was, 'What was all that about?'

'Ah, just to stir them up a bit, daughter, that's all,' he laughed.

'That was a bit cruel about FitzGerald's wife, wasn't it?' I said.

'Fuck them,' he replied.

Every day for a week, he went through the same routine. And they did take him to court for breach of the peace.

I remember him that morning, laughing as he got ready for court. Under his jeans, he wore Mickey Mouse boxer shorts he had sent my mother out to buy the day before. It was 14 April 1988. After an appearance at the Dublin District Court, the state had made an application to have him bound over to keep the peace. The state solicitor, Mr Donoghue, had said he had threatened his elderly neighbours, Mr and Mrs John Sisk of Cowper Road.

He appeared before District Justice Oliver Macklin. Seven garda witnesses told the court of the threats that Martin was making towards the elderly couple. There was no independent evidence of these threats except for the garda witnesses. The hearing was adjourned until 21 April.

I stood outside the Four Courts, waiting for Dad to come out. I'd brought my camera and the statements written out for the waiting press, which my father had sat up half the night typing. The statement for the press was advice for mothers on how to prevent cot death. He always believed that it was wrong to lay babies on their tummies in quiet, darkened rooms and he wrote down tips on the correct way to lay the baby and said to never let a baby overheat. I asked him why he was doing this. He said, 'Maybe one of the journalists will print it. You never know.' He was serious. Most of the journalists looked at the statement with bewilderment etched on their faces, then crumpled them up and threw them on the ground. To my knowledge, nobody printed it. Perhaps it was too bizarre; it definitely was not in keeping with his gangster image.

He came out of the court and the photographers rushed forward. He began to sing, 'I'm gonna sit right down and write myself a letter,' – off came the jacket

Martin Cahill in school,
aged 10.

Martin aged 15, before leaving
for Daingean.

Martin and Frances on their wedding day in March 1968, with
William Lawless and Mary Cahill.

Martin with his mother, Agnes, in 1980.

Agnes, aged 17

Martin's father, Paddy, down
at the docks in the 1970s.

Patrick 'Padser' Cahill, centre, with two friends (early 1980s).

From left: Anthony, Michael, Padser (on bike), Stephen Lawless, and Una.

Frances Cahill (nee Lawless) on far
right, with Hollyfield in the
background.

Frances Snr and Martin in 1975.

Frances Snr in Hollyfield shortly before the move to
Kevin Street.

Martin on his Harley Davidson in the 1970s.

Martin outside Hollyfield with, from left, Martin, Frances and a
young cousin, in 1975.

Frances Snr with Frances, Christopher and Martin
in 1977.

Martin with Frances, Martin and Christopher in 1975.

Frances Snr with the children
at Madame Tussaud's in 1974.

Frances with Martin in 1975.

Frances and Martin in Hollyfield in 1980.

Martin with baby Emma, Frances, Martin and Christopher, in front, in 1980.

– 'and make believe it came from you,' he sang, then dropped his trousers. 'Mickey Mouse!' he shouted, and the rest is history.

I clicked my camera as he stood there, arms outstretched. The Mickey Mouse boxer shorts were splashed across every newspaper the following day. 'The General' was now Ireland's godfather of crime with a sense of humour, making for colourful tabloid front pages. 'The General' as the joker and showman was born.

After he pulled the Mickey Mouse stunt for the cameras, the Special Branch pounced on him and arrested him. He turned and said, 'What? Oh yes, of course.' They frogmarched him into the Bridewell station behind the Four Courts, pulling his mask off and getting sly digs in because he couldn't see them in the mêlée. They were pulling his hair – the bit he had – and trying to expose his face for the cameras, but they didn't succeed. He was calling for his solicitor Gareth Sheehan, shouting out that he was being assaulted. The journalists loved every minute of it.

He refused to enter into a bond to keep the peace or put up two independent sureties of £500 each. He was also ordered to pay garda costs of £500. That was never going to happen. He would rather go to prison than pay. 'I'm not paying the money. I wouldn't pay it to the police, anyway,' he told reporters. 'They say everything I have is stolen and I wouldn't like to see them receiving stolen money.'

He claimed he was innocent anyway. He never told the Sisks that he was going to burn them out of their home – this was pure fabrication from the gardaí. He assured the Sisk family that despite what the gardaí were saying, they had nothing to fear from him.

Due to his failure to sign a bond to keep the peace, the District Court sentenced him to four months in prison. 'To be honest with you,' he told a reporter, 'I want to go on a diet. To be honest, I think it will do me good.' He was happy to do the time, but he would, of course, continue his battle.

He applied to the High Court for a judicial review of the District Court's decision to impose a sentence for failing to sign a bond to keep the peace. He was arguing against a fourteenth-century law which gives magistrates power to bind people over to the peace. His High Court action was grounded on the basis that the District Court order amounted to preventative justice. He also fought the constitutionality of the proceedings and of his detention. He would never give in to them – he fought everything.

The publicity around my father was in full swing after his appearance before the courts for breach of the peace. After he was released from Spike Island, he was transferred to Cork prison, then released with a train ticket home and a few bob in his pocket for the work he'd done while on the island. He told waiting reporters that he enjoyed his time on Spike Island with the seagulls. He'd grown a beard – his plan was to come off the island looking like Captain Birds Eye. He called it Treasure Island and said he felt like a pirate. 'A dose of prison does you good,' he told a reporter before he left. 'A lot of people need it.'

When asked what it was like to go back after all this time (the last time he'd been inside was during the 1970s) and how he felt about his new celebrity status, he replied, 'I'm thinking of running for the Dáil. I learned to count up to eleven while in prison. I reckon that qualified me to become a TD. If I go back in again, I'll learn to count to twelve. Who knows, I might make it as Taoiseach.'

They thought they could win the battle, but not that day. After being released, Martin told reporters, 'The gardaí can pull me in for anything, anytime, but I'm ready for round two with them.' No matter what they tried to do – whether it was trying to frame him, entrap him, build a case against him – they just couldn't do it. The frustration in the force was mounting.

— Part II
The Making of
'The General'

Chapter 5
Trial by Media

Everything changed after the **Today Tonight** programme in February 1988 put Martin in the spotlight.

While Martin was certainly known to the gardaí before then, he wouldn't have been widely known publicly. But after the programme aired, he became the focus of a lot more attention from the media as well as the government. There was a news story about him almost every week, turning 'Martin Cahill' into a household name, making him a celebrity criminal.

During the publicity that surrounded Martin, he received a lot of support from people urging him to stand up to the authorities and never falter. Many people admired his success in overcoming the pressure of the gardaí. He had letters and cards of support from all over Ireland and beyond. The amount of cards that came through the letterbox at Christmastime from prisoners all over Ireland was unreal, some with only 'Martin, Rathmines' written for an address. One birthday card from Gartree Prison reads like a who's who of famous convicts, including the Kray twins, the Guilford Four and the Birmingham Six. My own favourite is from Paddy

Joe Hill of the Guilford Four, who wrote, 'From one innocent man to another.'

*

The RTÉ **Today Tonight** current affairs programme aired in February 1988 on organised crime in Dublin, featuring so-called Dublin underworld criminals, was a blatant disregard of the civil liberties of those featured on the programme, as these people were named and put in the public eye without due process. The chairman of the Council for Civil Liberties at the time, Kadar Asmal, was very critical of the programme, saying it amounted to a 'public trial' and questioning whether a person in the programme would now be able to get a fair trial if they were ever charged.

Martin had no presumption of innocence after that – everyone's mind was made up, Martin Cahill must be guilty. To say it was a trial by media would be an understatement. The programme's front man, Brendan O'Brien, hosted a ninety-minute interview with my father on a Dublin street with a garda surveillance team sitting close by. The programme was heavily edited and the questions and answers put across in a haphazard way. O'Brien could be seen laughing away at the jokes my father was pulling.

The whole broadcast was a fiasco. It had full approval from the Garda Commissioner, Eamonn Doherty, who was looking for political and public support in continuing with the impractical, costly surveillance that followed Martin Cahill everywhere. The maker of the programme, Eugene Murray, a brother of the Attorney General at the time, John Murray, had the go-ahead to do the show and start the ball rolling. It was a publicity stunt from start to finish.

The Dáil erupted after the programme was broadcast, with politicians such as Des O'Malley, the leader of the Progressive Democrats, mentioning Martin Cahill by name and saying what an outrage it was that this man could use the system as he was. O'Malley even went so far as to suggest that the low-income people of this country would derive some consolation in the knowledge that their tax money was keeping the likes of Martin Cahill in dole payments. This disgraceful attack from a party leader was quickly stopped by the Ceann Comhairle and O'Malley was advised to stop mentioning individuals' names that were not in the house.

The highly edited show was biased and totally one sided. But the whole thing failed. The reason the show was aired was to put Martin in the spotlight. Martin knew that the garda strategy was to cut him off from all his sources of money so he would go out and be reckless. They tried to ostracise him by harassing any associates of his. But this didn't work either. They were letting the country know that if they couldn't prosecute, then they would persecute instead.

We were sitting at home waiting for the show to
come on. My father had said it was possible that he
would be the focus of the programme. He had told us
how a reporter, Brendan O'Brien, came up to him on
the street out of the blue outside the Labour Exchange
on Werburgh Street and asked him questions about
the surveillance and about robberies in the city. This
fella wanted some sort of admission from my father
that he was the culprit behind the Beit art robbery two
years previously.

We watched the programme and he got a great
laugh out of it, especially when his friend Christie
Dutton began pushing and lunging at the camera,
telling O'Brien to fuck off. Martin found it even
funnier when Christie came down to the house and
said, 'What'll we do, Martin? All the fucking
attention. I don't like it.'

Christie left the house that evening a much more
relaxed man. Martin had made him realise that this
was nothing, that the law – a word he used for the
police – had put the journalists onto the story. It was
as much of a joke as the police themselves sitting on
the wall. Nothing to worry about.

The media attention he received after the **Today
Tonight** programme was overwhelming. Joining the
ranks of the detectives now was an irritating little
posse of journalists eager to get on the bandwagon.
The police found they came in useful as a propaganda
tool and used them to build many of the stories that

circulated at that time, which they presumably did to put increasing pressure on Martin and his day-to-day activities. At the beginning, one of us might complain about the 'crazy reporters' that hung around the corners who would confront you, sometimes scaring the living daylights out of you. But Dad would just tell us to ignore them and act as if they weren't there. 'They'll get bored soon and go,' he would laugh.

Journalists would hang around outside of our house, but when Martin emerged with his balaclava covering his face, they didn't rush to surround him – they were slightly shy about approaching him outside the house and instead would take photos from a distance. I believe they were really scared of him. No one but Veronica Guerin would actually approach him. However, the media constantly sent letters asking him for interviews and photo sessions – they were obsessed with seeing his face. Countless efforts were made to try to catch him without the mask on. He was stalked by vans with blacked-out windows. These weren't the gardaí – they were on the other side of the road – these were the newspapers trying to get a photo. They never got one. The only photo of him that appeared in one of the newspapers was of him at my sister's communion. This photo was stolen from our house by the gardaí during a raid, who then handed it over to the newspaper.

Nothing could faze him. He never worried or cared that these people were making up some crazy story about him. One story came out that he and my mother went to orgies at the weekend and that he would sometimes send her out on the game for a bit of extra cash. My mother would squint in disbelief at some of the tales, but he would laugh and brush it off – though he did say he was going to burn down the **Sunday World** building (or as he called it, the **Garda Papers**). He never really cared about the press or what they said about him, as he saw them merely as an extended voice of the gardaí.

'So what?' was Martin's attitude towards the **Today Tonight** programme.

Yet there were other repercussions from the programme. Martin Cahill was not only denounced from the Dáil, his social welfare payments were cut off, as well as those of some close family members who were in receipt of a welfare payment.

It was suggested that Martin had admitted that he worked as a private detective during the interview, which resulted in his dole payments being cut off. What he really said was that his friend had a detective agency and he only worked if there was any work to be had, but there never was. Martin later said in an interview, 'Since everywhere we go, the gardaí go, we can offer an armed garda escort for the movement of large amounts of cash.' It also advertised that profits from the company would go to charity. It was a joke, really, just another dig at the gardaí.

After a so-called investigation into his means of income, it turned out that he wasn't a man of means after all – well, not on paper anyway – but the rules did not apply where he was concerned. The Department of Welfare refused to give him back his social welfare payment. After his appeal to the department, stories of him intimidating high-ranking officials who worked in the department began to circulate. All he wanted was for the department to give him a reason as to why he wasn't entitled to get a payment even though he had no visible means of income. They could not give him any answers.

*

One particular story which was circulated by the media – fuelled by the gardaí, no doubt – was the tale of Martin having an affair with one of his wife's sisters.

This so-called affair was supposed to be common knowledge amongst the family and my mother actually shrieked with laughter when certain tabloids stated that they had a **ménage à trois** going; I'm not even sure she knew what it meant.

The story went that he was having an affair with her sister and was the father of her four or five children. He was supposed to be living his night-time life with her at Swan Grove and spending the days with my mother in Cowper Downs. The truth was that the house he stayed in some nights in Ranelagh was actually my mother's house, which she paid for with her own money at the knock-down price of

£19,000 when Dublin Corporation offered tenants this chance to buy as part of Dublin's millennium celebrations.

My mother's mother lived in a flat on Tom Kelly Road in Dublin. She was getting old and unwell, so my mother moved her into the Swan Grove house to look after her. Some of my grandmother's middle-aged children never really had lives of their own, and two of her daughters stayed in Swan Grove to help look after her. This story that my aunt lived with us and was carrying on some sort of relationship for all to see was complete and utter rubbish. I've said that I wasn't going to start denying all the allegations, but in this case, I see no other way than to offer this outright rebuttal. He did not ever display any sort of disrespect towards my mother or his children; he was not the type. This was one part of the Martin Cahill saga that could have hurt us, but we are made of stronger stuff and my father's attitude of not giving a damn what tabloids say about the family rubbed off on us, to great effect.

*

But Martin could also use the media to his own advantage. In 1990, Martin appeared before the court on a charge of dangerous driving, obstruction and breach of the peace. The garda who'd arrested him asked for Martin to be remanded in custody for a psychiatric evaluation because of Martin's behaviour when he'd been arrested that day, stripping off on

Palmerstown Road and later stripping naked in his cell at Rathmines garda station. 'It was a very hot day. I just took off my shirt,' Martin said in court. He went along to the assessment and told the psychologist that he was a bird. The psychologist told him to leave.

After he appeared before the court again, Martin left the court in a white gown like the ones they wear in mental institutions and a bird's nest on his head, complete with birds and straw inside, and the words 'one flew under the cuckoo's nest' written down the front of the gown. He had gotten my brother, Martin Jnr., to make his little get-up the night before. He played up to the waiting reporters and photographers, asking them, 'Is this the Liffey? Is this a swan? Are you a chicken?' He then got on a bicycle and cycled down the quays outside the Four Courts, blowing through a duck decoy and asking passers-by if they were swans or pigeons and saying, 'I'm a cuckoo and I'm going off to meet my friends,' with photographers and children chasing after him on his bike. We sat at home and watched it on the news and had a laugh. That's what it was all about – he was showing his contempt for the courts and the gardaí.

*

Another thing the **Today Tonight** programme did was to start Ireland's 'gangland scourge' thing. Dublin was now this hotbed of crime run by the evil Martin Cahill, the 'Godfather of Crime'. This kind of journalism, fuelled by garda hearsay and innuendo, resulted in the emergence of the 'investigative crime reporter'. The tabloid press didn't really kick off in Ireland until the early to mid-1980s, and Martin Cahill and his type were what they needed. The mythical so-called circle that criminals operated within was to be infiltrated by a posse of dynamic and brave crime writers that emerged from the bowels of the tabloids.

The most persistent of the lot was the journalist Veronica Guerin, who wrote for the **Sunday Business Post** and the **Sunday Tribune** and, later, the **Sunday Independent**. The first time she came to our house in 1988, I answered the door. She was very pleasant and introduced herself as Veronica.

'Hi, is your dad about?' she asked as if she was a friend of the family.

'Eh, no, sorry. He doesn't talk to reporters, I'm afraid,' I replied and began to slowly close the door. She stepped forward and put her hand on the door.

'Frances, is it?'

'Yes, I'm Frances, but you're wasting your time. He won't talk to you, so if you don't mind...' I tried to close the door again, but again she gently pushed it back open.

'Listen, I only want to ask him a couple of questions. Or maybe you would like to give me a little help?'

I laughed and shut the door over, saying, 'No, sorry, we can't talk to anybody.' I looked through the glass spy hole in the door to see if she was gone, but she was still there, staring at the door and looking as if she was wondering what to do next.

Dad passed me in the hallway. 'What's up?'

'Da, there's some journalist at the door and she won't go away.' He looked through the spy hole and saw her standing there, as if she was waiting for a bus.

'Watch this,' he said. He left me standing at the door and went and put on his mask. He opened the door, and before she could say anything, he took her by the arm and marched her to the gate.

'Mr Cahill, just a couple of questions.' She was turning to him, pleading for him to talk to her, but he didn't say a word, he just put her on the outside of the gate and closed it.

'Mr Cahill, why the mask?' she asked, as if the question was something she wondered about personally.

'Go away out of that now,' he laughed to himself as he closed the door.

She still stood there as he quietly closed the door, a big hopeful smile on her face. This was the first – and for a long time, the last – Martin would be seeing of Veronica, until he gave word one day about a year after her first visit to the house that she was to meet him in the house at Cowper Downs. However, Veronica pursued the rest of the family relentlessly. Then one day she stopped calling.

She had found someone that gave her the time of day – John Traynor, an associate of my father's.

Traynor was a small-time con man, a second-hand car dealer, a cheques man. Martin never really did anything with John – he never trusted him; he knew what he was. Traynor was a bit of a talker in a wheeler-dealer sort of way. Veronica had found her link into the so-called underworld.

*

The summer of 1984 saw a burglary that was to torment An Garda Síochána and the Director of Public Prosecutions for a very long time: sensitive case files were stolen from the DPP's office.

Martin knew that there actually wasn't much to the files. They didn't contain a lot, mainly gruesome pictures of murdered people. He stole the files to annoy the gardaí, nothing more. He wanted to show them he could do whatever he wanted to, but everything he did was for a specific reason.

Amongst these files was a file on my father's brother, Patrick. In December 1986, Patrick was stabbed to death by Anthony Quinn in Ballyfermot, where they lived. Patrick and Quinn were having an argument that had been going on for months. It came to a tragic end one night in the Quinns' garden. Pat, who was paralysed after a motorcycle accident that had also involved my father and uncle, John Lawless, had been knocked out by Quinn. He lay unconscious on the ground while Quinn went into his house and got a knife, returned to where Pat lay, straddled over him and stabbed him ten times. His self-defence plea was accepted by the courts.

Martin sent people after Quinn, but it was more of a chase than a hunt, it was more him telling Quinn to go disappear. Nobody wanted Quinn to go down for Pat's murder. What happened, happened. Nothing would bring Patrick back and Martin certainly didn't want the gardaí thinking that he needed them and the courts to give his family justice for the murder of his brother. If he needed any justice, he would deal with it himself.

*

Veronica Guerin's death in 1996 brought everything back to me. The manner in which she was executed bore uncanny similarities to my father's death: shot dead in broad daylight through the window of her car, the murderers making a hasty getaway through the Dublin traffic on a motorbike. I knew exactly what her family was going through – the disbelief, the confusion. However, the reasons behind their two deaths were very different.

Veronica had found someone to talk 'crime' with. After knocking on many doors and after many dodgy meetings in dingy old Dublin pubs, she found John Traynor. Some would call Traynor a friend of my father's, and it's true that he was quite close to our family. When we were kids, we looked on John as an uncle. He was always giving all the kids tenners each, when in those days 10p was the usual pocket money. He always wore a shirt and tie and I thought he must have been an important businessman. In reality, 'Uncle' John was a small-time con man, someone who was always willing to do you a favour but equally willing to do you out of a few bob. John felt that Martin liked him and trusted him to an extent, but Martin never really brought him in on any business he personally had to do. All the same, Traynor was handy to have around and a genuinely likeable sort of chap.

I remember my father sending me to London to give John a message and I'll never forget the con man in action. He was crying the poor mouth and pleading with me to return and tell my father how hard up he was; the guy even had matchsticks holding his cuffs together. Veronica obviously didn't see him for what he was – a crooked little used car dealer who had as much success in getting my father to talk to journalists as he had in getting Veronica into bed. For John was a ladies' man – although happily married for years to a respectable middle-class woman who sat at home in their tidy house with her embroidery to keep her busy, he always had a girlfriend.

There was one thing Veronica wanted from Martin, and that was to get her hands on the stolen DPP files. She was obsessed with these files and her conversations with Traynor mainly centred around getting in with Martin. Of course, this was like trying to get a politician to admit to having an offshore investment account. Veronica persisted with hounding Traynor for information and he gave her little stories and dribbles of information concerning some of the files.

Martin told Traynor to tell Guerin to fuck off.

'Martin, this bitch won't leave me alone. She'll do anything for a story,' Traynor said.

They both laughed at this, but my father was serious. 'John, don't get involved with these gossip-mongers. They try to make money off your back, that's all they do.'

Martin's attitude towards the gutter press was well known. He had no time for any of them. The only person he had any respect for was the barrister Michael O'Higgins, who wrote for **Magill** magazine. Martin was impressed with the articles he wrote about civil liberties and his criticism of the abuse by gardaí in their use of the Offences against the State Act and the erosion of civil liberties in Ireland by the state in general. He found O'Higgins to be fair in his writings, and O'Higgins was fully aware of the flip side of the coin regarding the gardaí. The tabloid journalists, on the other hand, were mainly fuelled by the gardaí and the majority of their articles have been one sided and biased in favour of An Garda Síochána.

So it came as quite a surprise to me to arrive home from work one evening at Cowper Downs to find Veronica Guerin sitting on our sofa with a cup of tea and my father sitting with his hands clasped tightly together and listening to her with an air of great interest.

Veronica sat there with her knees crossed and her arms folded, her body language suggesting that she was nervous to be in our house talking to my father, the very man she had wanted to talk to for years. He put her at ease when he began to explain to her that he could understand where reporters were coming from and he knew that they all had livings to earn, but he felt that she was wasting her time trying to build up a huge story about him being this big gangster. He told her not to listen to the gardaí building up the stories about him. Likewise, he said her exposure of the poxy Dublin drug dealers would only make their egos bigger.

She started to push him with questions about convicted criminal John Gilligan and George 'The Penguin' Mitchell, men she would go on to write about as being two of the main players on the Dublin drugs scene (Gilligan went on to attack and threaten her in September 1995 when she tried to interview him). Martin just smiled and said, 'Ah, come on now, don't start interviewing me, this is not what I wanted to see you about.'

My father never had anything to do with John Gilligan, a man he found to be repulsive. I recall Martin grabbing him by the scruff of the neck and booting him down our garden path and out the gate. Given the manner in which he had ejected him from our house, I figured Martin thought of him as a cheeky little bollox, his 'get the fuck out' actions speaking for themselves.

'Listen now, would you not be better off reporting on the real criminals in this country?' he said. Veronica tried to interrupt, but he raised his hand and, tilting his head towards her, urged her to listen carefully.

'What about all the child abuse in the country? What about the pervert priests being allowed to carry on raping kids and all this being hidden by the bishops? Why don't you look into stories like that?'

'Martin, I want all of those stories, but in this country I have to be careful what I say, especially about the Church.'

'What about Father Molloy and the cover-up of the killing? What about that Judge Roe – why was he allowed to acquit Flynn after only a couple of hours? They're all members of the Turf Club, they're all buddies. What about the backhanders?'

Veronica unfolded her arms. 'Do you have information about the killing? Can you show me the files?' She sat there wide eyed.

'Now come on, I'm not showing anybody anything and I'm not saying anything. I'm just suggesting to you that stories about some of the real criminals in this country need to be told, and I think you have the balls to tell them.'

Veronica smiled and sat back in the chair. Her confidence was growing.

The killing of the priest Fr Niall Molloy in 1985 was of huge interest to Veronica. She believed that the DPP file on the case would have details that had never

been revealed, and she wanted that file. The story
went that Fr Molloy, a horse racing enthusiast, was
found dead in the blood-splattered bedroom of
businessman and stud owner Richard Flynn and his
wife, Therese Flynn, in Kilcoursey House in Clara,
County Offaly. My father recalled that the priest's
head had been bashed in with a statue of a horse,
information that allegedly came from the DPP's file on
the case. Therese Flynn, a keen horsewoman, and Fr
Molloy shared an interest in the horse racing business
and the family was well known in the high-society life
that flourished around the horse racing circuits of
Ireland. The rumours that circulated at the time were
that the priest and Therese were having an affair and
that Richard Flynn caught them in bed together on the
night of his daughter's society wedding. Richard Flynn
was charged with manslaughter after he told gardaí
that the priest had attacked him and that he had
reacted in self-defence.

Trial Judge Frank Roe, the president of the Circuit
Court, acquitted Flynn when it was suggested from the
state pathologist's evidence that he could not rule out
that the priest could have had heart failure and banged
his head on the bedpost when he fell. According to my
father, the evidence in the files suggests that the
injuries sustained by the priest go slightly beyond
banging one's head on a bedpost.

Veronica was hooked. He told her that he could
arrange for her to view sensitive files if she would

begin reporting stories on the Catholic Church and corrupt gardaí and politicians. He told her that he could give her leads only if she agreed to swing the pendulum both ways.

She agreed.

*

Apart from this story, Veronica's interest in the evergrowing Dublin drugs trade was overwhelming. This seedy world was dominated by the type of people who would run your granny over and reverse over her again to make sure she wouldn't finger them. She was fascinated with them – not just the stories that were generated out of the hype that the journalists built around these figures, but the lifestyle these people led. Most of them were police informers who used their association with Martin to give them a reputation as a hard guy. They were known by their nicknames, either real ones given to them by their associates or the police, or else names crime journalists such as Veronica made up for them – 'The Monk', 'The Penguin' and 'The Viper', to name a few – to circumvent Irish libel laws. But they didn't just give them nicknames – they also gave these pathetic nobodies the big heads they needed to continue with their evil trade.

After the meeting with Guerin in Cowper Downs, my father didn't have any further meetings with her. Once again, she began again calling to the house, only to be constantly told 'Sorry, he isn't home' or 'No, he still doesn't talk to reporters'.

'But will you tell him it's Veronica?' she pleaded as the door would gently close.

What she didn't realise was that Martin often acted on a whim. He decided one day to have her up and then quickly forgot about her. He was waiting for the stories of the paedophile priests and the bishops who protected them to break.

Guerin went on to expose Bishop Comiskey, Bishop of Ferns, who was alleged to have known about paedophile priest Fr Sean Fortune. Fr Fortune's deplorable activities in his diocese were covered up by the bishop, who moved him around and continued to allow him to have contact with children. This was the catalyst for the unravelling of the high-flying bishop's career and the beginning of the end for the veil of secrecy surrounding the Church, whose cover-ups and hypocrisy concerning the vicious child rapists that continued to preach the word of God from the pulpits was also exposed.

Before Veronica's death, she was preparing to run the full story on Fr Molloy and the whole sordid business of his violent death. She was also giving An Garda Síochána a hard time in the press about their handling of the fatal shooting of Detective Garda Jerry McCabe during an attempted post office robbery in June 1996, just a few weeks before her own death. Veronica didn't have many friends in the end – she was going after everybody. The story she was going to tell was never told. The mystery surrounding the case goes on and will forever be buried in the thick, musty annals of Irish scandals. As will other stories.

My father would have loved to have read the story. And he would have hated to see her die the way she did. She was a mother, and to leave a young child without a mother was a deplorable, cowardly act.

*

On the day of my father's death, I wearily opened the door to another journalist. It was Veronica. She handed me a bunch of roses. I closed the door on her for the last time. My mother took the flowers and threw them into the skip that sat outside on the footpath, where it joined the other bunches of tacky flowers that had been arriving at the house all day long from journalists and editors. Two years later, journalists and editors across the city would be sending Veronica's family the same tributes.

Chapter 6
Life with the Tango Squad

Martin sat at our kitchen table looking out the window. It was a freezing January morning in 1988, the kind of morning you wanted to stay in bed. He sat in his coat with a teacup pressed to his lips, blowing into the cup and letting the steam warm his face.

'Jesus, Da, light the bleeding fire, will ye?' I said as I passed by him and picked up the kettle, raising my gaze to settle on the detective sitting on the cold, hard wall at the end of the garden, wrapped up tight and freezing. We had gotten so used to them at this stage that we rarely mentioned them, but we always kept an eye on them to make sure they weren't up to anything.

'It's about time you're up,' Da said. 'Look at the time. Half the day is gone, for God's sake.'

I looked at the clock: 10:00 a.m. 'What?' I said, irritated by his remark. 'I'm up ages,' I grumbled to myself as he walked over to me, pulling on his cap and zipping up his jacket.

'Half the day is gone,' he said in my ear. 'Don't be lazy.'

'Ah, shut up, will ye?' I moaned, pouring out the tea. He laughed and walked out the back door. The dick sitting on the wall stirred a bit, took his hands from his pockets and pulled his hood tighter around his face. Martin walked down the garden towards the pigeon loft. The pigeons stirred to life when they heard him get closer. When he went into the garden, the birds would all fly around him, landing on his arms if he stretched them out. I watched him disappear into the loft, then the dick on the wall settled back into his place, put his hands back in his pockets and the birds settled down.

Whenever Martin was on the move, someone or something was either scrambling after him, following him or staring at him. When he got in his car, eyes watched him and detectives crept after him. Neighbours would nervously look at him, then turn away and look surprised when he would say hello or nod good morning. But he always had a relaxed air about him; he rarely did anything quickly. He walked slowly, with a distinctive sway, a manner instantly recognisable even from a distance.

*

The Minister for Justice, Gerard Collins, and Garda Commissioner Eamonn Doherty decided to set up a special unit of sixty detectives to watch Dublin's top criminals. The Tango Squad was a group of mainly young detectives, some just out of uniform, put together by Commissioner Doherty in 1988 to act as a surveillance team that was to follow Martin Cahill

– aka Tango One, their code name for him – and his associates twenty-four hours a day, seven days a week. The tactics they employed were supposed to have come from the example of the surveillance team that were on the Kray twins in England during the 1960s. This particular type of intimidation and harassment was meant to make Martin slip up, make mistakes and become reckless. It didn't work.

*

Once, at a funeral of a family member in 1989, my father hung back to have a yap with the gravedigger, a fella he knew well. I called Da to leave: 'Are ye right, Da, we're going.'

'Yeah, Frances, hang on,' he called over to me, then turned to the gravedigger. 'Now no robbin' the brass off the coffin,' he quietly joked.

'Ah, Martin, we won't,' the fella laughed. 'See ye now.'

'Not too soon, I hope,' Martin replied, smiling.

We walked out of the cemetery together and I linked his arm. 'They don't really take the brass off the coffins, do they?' I asked, squirming at the idea.

'Course they do. For fuck's sake, what's the point in burying it? They sell it back to the funeral homes. You know what they do at coppers' funerals, don't you?'

'What?' I asked apprehensively.

'Well, I know that at certain coppers' funerals, the

coffin is opened and – this is no lie – they bash the corpse's face in with the shovel.'

'No way, Da, that's not true.' I looked at him.

'I'm telling ye,' he smiled, 'it's true.'

*

People took up most of my father's day – people and pigeons. The only time he seemed to have to himself was after midnight, when he went out. Most nights as the family was winding down, getting ready for bed, he was putting on his jacket and his trilby hat to leave for the night.

He would go out for a 'mooch around' and always brought his pocket torch. Usually a 'mooch around' meant going out for a walk on his own, then a trip to the video shop. Sometimes he'd get a takeaway, then he would either come back to Cowper Downs or stay in my mother's house in Swan Grove in Ranelagh, the house we'd transferred to from Kevin Street. When the Cowper Downs house was bought, my mother moved my grandmother into the house in Ranelagh, so some nights Martin would stretch out on the sofa for cat naps. He never slept for more than four hours at a time. During the day he would catch a couple of hours in the afternoon.

His routine was fairly regular, but no matter how routinely he led his life, the gardaí were a constant presence that lurked on our back wall, that mumbling you could always hear as you hung out the washing or folded up the deckchairs in the evening. You could always hear them whispering or the muffled sound of a police radio in the inside pockets of their Berber jackets. But he could always get away from them when he wanted to – he could shake them off like the pigeon feathers stuck in his hair. And they knew it.

My father had many ways of leaving the house undetected. For instance, he and Christopher could walk into his loft under the watchful gaze of three or four surveillance fellas sitting on the wall. They would sit there all day thinking that he was in there cleaning the loft. They could hear them scraping the floors, pouring seed and whistling, but unbeknownst to them, Martin was actually cycling down Palmerston Road on his bicycle, heading off to meet someone, leaving Christopher alone to do the chores. Inside the loft, cleverly concealed behind the shelves on which his beloved pigeons sat, was a hole he had carved into the wall of the loft that led to an overgrown area between the loft and the fence next door. He would quietly crawl under the bushes to a hole he had dug under the fence. Once under the fence, he would crawl under the neatly pruned hedge at the end of our neighbour's garden. Once he got through the neighbour's garden, he could then emerge and hop over the fence into the next garden until eventually he sauntered unnoticed out onto a footpath, the police still on the wall, thinking he was still pottering around with his pigeons. Sometimes the police would be too busy chatting amongst themselves or racing up and down the estate on police motorbikes to notice him just strolling out the front door and around the corner.

Also unbeknownst to the police, he had a stash of about fifteen cars, mainly old bangers, placed around the city. These cars were all taxed and insured in other people's names so that they were all legit and above board. If he needed to get somewhere by car undetected, he would use a car and always put it back in the same area, but never in the same exact place, so people in the vicinity wouldn't complain to the gardaí about cars left outside their homes for days, sometimes months, on end.

Most of the time, though, he just walked out the front door, the police snoozing in their cars.

*

Martin's so-called battle with the Irish police force was a farce, a joke. For example, in September 1983, the gardaí discovered that guns were being taken from the Garda Technical Bureau on St Johns Road in Kilmainham. Martin had been getting into the premises for a long time. The place was so badly secured that he would drop in, take what he wanted, use it, then take it back.

He treated the whole lot of them with an air of nonchalance. He didn't care if they tailed him. Even if he lived to be a hundred years old, their presence would never mean much to him. He knew that he could carry on his life as normal whether they sat on walls or sat beside him in restaurants. This behaviour never bothered him. He knew it and they knew it. If he wanted to give them the slip for a few hours or a few days, he could. He once took a trip to the UK for the weekend while the surveillance team perched on the wall were none the wiser. Their presence took on a more farcical note the more this went on, and the cries from the Oireachtas about how much taxpayers' money was being wasted on these measures fell on deaf ears.

Another one of his tactics for giving them the slip was his vast amount of disguises. He had at least twenty wigs of all different colours and styles, several different moustaches and a box full of spectacles. He even had sets of false teeth of the type used on film sets, which could give his face a totally different look.

His use of disguises was sometimes a great amusement to us. He would stop you in the street and ask for directions while dressed in a perfect blue suit, gleaming white shirt and silk tie. A wig and glasses or a moustache would complete the get-up. He looked like a doctor or an accountant and he could put on a brilliant accent, sometimes sounding like an English lord. He would then reveal to you later on that it was him you'd been talking to in the street earlier. His disguises really were that good.

One thing he could not get away with was dressing up as a woman – not with his legs, anyway. But he was excellent as a tramp. He recalled how nobody looks at a tramp. He could lie down across the pavement and people would step over him or walk around him, but never look at him. Tramps could get on with whatever they had to do and no one would pay a blind bit of notice. He would even carry a bottle in a brown bag and swig water from it. Uniformed gardaí on the beat would sometimes tell him to move on if he was taking up space on a bench somewhere, but even that was rare. Sometimes, if he had to meet a friend to talk, his friend would also rough himself up a bit and act like a wino so no one took any notice of the two bums having their conversation in the park.

The gardaí could not understand how he always gave them the slip. Little did they know he was out getting on with his life, sometimes in a priest's suit. I nearly swallowed my tongue with laughter when he sauntered into the living room one day dressed as a priest with a perfect black wig and asked me without a glimmer of humour, 'How do I look?' On another occasion he told me that he had attended a garda ball in disguise, and none of the gardaí had recognised him.

Given that Martin was followed closely by detectives from the early 1970s up until his death in 1994, he was bound to devise ways of giving the police the slip. The gardaí have always been baffled as to how he could constantly evade them. Sometimes they uncovered a wig or a false moustache during a raid, but always presumed he used them for robberies.

One time, his friend Christie Dutton went out to rob a security van dressed as a woman, pram and all. Instead of a baby inside the pram was a doll, and underneath the doll was a sawn-off shotgun. The target was a security van carrying money into a bank. Christie walked to the bank, an auld wan's scarf wrapped tightly around his head. He made for a comical sight, but looked every inch the mother pushing the pram. When he got up to the security van, he reached into the pram and pulled out the shotgun. The startled security guard handed him the bag. He put the money into the pram, tucked the gun back under the blanket and made off. No one was hurt and the robbery was a success. Martin got a great laugh out of that.

*

The heat rose from the footpath in a haze. It was one of those glorious Irish summer days. The air was warm and still and everything outside had a tepid, pastel glow. I was gazing out of the upstairs window, feeling sleepy as the sun shone on my face, when the first car screeched to a halt outside the garden gate. More cars pulled up and around twenty gardaí hopped from the cars and ran up our garden towards the door. I called out to Dad, who was busy out in the pigeon lofts.

'Da, I think it's a raid! There's loads of coppers banging down the door.'

He came out of the loft as they came running down the side lane, screeching out his name in their thick country accents: 'Martin Cahill, you're under arrest!'

He slowly walked towards them, covering his face with his hand. 'Where's the search warrant?' He looked up to me then. 'Frances, call Gareth Sheehan.'

They took him by the arm and led him down the side lane.

'Where's your warrant? You're on private property, this arrest is unlawful.'

One of the gardaí waved a warrant under his nose and bundled him in the back of the car. They sped out of the estate. A few hours later he would be back in the house, writing out his complaint to the Garda Complaints Board, even though it never got him anywhere.

My father had been making complaints about the gardaí harassing and threatening his family from his garden wall over a long period of time. The abusive insults and threats came from the gardaí on a daily basis. They would throw beer cans at us and spit down on top of the children as they played in the garden. They would empty sacks of rubbish over the wall and call my mother a slut as she picked it up. Most of the time she would leave it, unless it was too close to the back door and we would be tripping over the bottles and cans the gardaí had hurled at the house.

Most of the surveillance team wore masks or grew long beards so we couldn't pick them out or identify them when they were carrying out unlawful activities. One of the detectives told my father that he would never pick him out because he had a twin. While in court on the breach of the peace hearing in 1988, this garda went state witness against Martin. When Martin's barrister, Adrian Hardiman, produced photographs of the gardaí on the wall with ski masks covering their faces and asked him if he told Mr Cahill that he would never pick him out because he had a twin, the garda denied it. When asked how Mr Cahill would even know he had a twin if he hadn't told him, the garda couldn't answer.

The gardaí denied harassing my family. We would take photographs of them urinating into the garden and throwing rubbish over the wall. Martin had a surveillance camera installed to the rear of the house which recorded their activities. He could see them opening the traps on the pigeon lofts and putting our neighbour's cats loose into the lofts to savage the birds. Nothing ever came of our documentation. But again, nothing they did could bother him. He just hit back.

*

My father had a wide circle of friends and acquaintances. Most people got to know him through friends recommending them to him or through old family friends. Most days, there would seldom be fewer than ten callers to the house. Talking to all these people kept my father very busy and he would often carry on with his daily chores of tending to his racing pigeons. He always had a warm welcome for most people and could chat for hours on end, laughing one minute, then whispering the next. I would often wonder what they could possibly be discussing, but eavesdropping was next to impossible. He had an amazing ability to engage in discussion with a person in a way that if he wanted to prevent other people in the room from hearing his conversation, he used a form of sign language and gestures. This was also necessary because of the bugging devices that were planted around the house.

My mother discovered one of these devices behind the skirting board in the living room one day. She was a little shocked and angry, knowing the police were listening to everything in the house, but my father laughed and put it back where she'd found it. He told my mother to relax and be careful what she said aloud in the future.

He was going to use the bugs for his own gain – he would successfully confuse the police using this method of communication. For his own amusement, he would often openly discuss a robbery that was going down on a particular day and details such as the place and time would be confided to…the dog. He'd put his finger to his mouth. 'Shhh,' he'd whisper, putting his hand over our mouths to muffle the laughter. We all knew the police were listening and probably getting excited at the prospect of catching Martin red handed.

'The cells in police stations are all bugged. They are listening in on all conversations between you and your solicitor. Don't open your fucking mouth, I'm telling ya,' he'd say. They also had our phone tapped and every room in the Cowper Downs house. They were listening in on everything.

After my mother found the bugs in the house and Martin told her to put them back, we knew where we stood. He would test the phone bug by arranging a meeting with a friend, giving the details of the place and time. He would then slip out of the house in disguise and watch the police come to the spot and try to spy on him to see what he was up to. We were told to never give out any personal information over the phone. Basically, if you had anything to say that you didn't want the Harcourt station to know about, don't say it over the damn phone. This sounds like we had to be paranoid, to say the least, but it was accepted as a part of life and we all took it in our stride.

*

During the surveillance in the 1980s, the police were using well-known informers to try to trap Martin. He was wise to this, and instead of distancing himself from an informer, he used the person and kept them close. He used informers just as much as the police did.

Martin's decision to keep the game going in this way was sometimes frustrating to his brother Eddie. Eddie hated everything about these people – they have no scruples and a police informer would never be anything but a rat. One such informer – I'll call him 'The Rat' – was a well-known crook around Dublin, but it was common knowledge that he was a rat. 'This bollox is a very dangerous person,' Martin told me of 'The Rat'. 'He wouldn't think twice about letting you get shot by these bastards,' meaning the police. But the pretence was allowed to continue. I still find it difficult to understand how my father could put up with this person in our house, knowing full well what he was.

But to Martin, it was like a cat playing with a mouse. These people would be allowed into our house, where Martin would sit and chat with them for hours. He would use them to leak back rumours to the gardaí. Eddie always said that these informers would use their association with Martin for their own gain, but Martin used them just as much as they were being used by the police. He particularly loved to infuriate the police by 'turning' the informer. To 'turn' an informer means totally turning them around so that they would find the faith, as such, in Martin and no longer work for the gardaí. This was a huge body blow for the gardaí, and realising that he was capable of this was another reason for the police to despise him. All the same, an informer can never be trusted and Martin never went too far in his dealings with these people. It was just another way to beat the police at their own game.

*

The gardaí began to harass Martin's children more and more. Martin Jr. and Christopher got it worse than me. The gardaí hated that none of Martin's children were involved in any kind of criminal activity. When only a teenager, Christopher was beaten on Rathmines Road by two off-duty gardaí. He was constantly being harassed and poked at. They wanted to get him for a criminal conviction, another tag to use against my father. They didn't succeed. No amount of provocation could make our family fall into their traps.

Anywhere we went, anything we did, the gardaí weren't far behind. But we knew this was all part of the game our father had told us about. We knew life was going to be tough, what with constantly being harassed and ridiculed because of who our father was. We saw from a very early age exactly what our father was fighting against, and from a very early age we have been proud of him. He stood up for what he believed in. He was our hero.

One time, when I was nineteen, it was my turn to be on the receiving end of the garda harassment. I had started working in a newsagent in Churchtown and the owner sacked me because detectives had paid him a visit before I showed up for work one evening. They told him that I was Martin Cahill's daughter – 'You know, the General.' He told me not to put my bag down, to just get out of the shop. I left. The dicks were sitting outside the shop and shouted over, 'Go home, Cahill, you little prostitute. Your aul' fella's a cunt.'

I smiled over at them. They didn't bother me. I was waiting for it anyway. When I got back home and inside our hall door, though, my emotions took over. When my da turned around in the hall and said, 'Frances, I thought you were going to work,' I didn't want to tell him; I thought he would feel bad. The tears began to fall. 'What's wrong with ye, daughter?'

I told him what had happened, and about the detectives sitting outside and laughing at me. I quickly told him that it wasn't the police that bothered me – he would have killed me, you weren't allowed to be bothered by the police, and besides, I was well used to it – it was the shopkeeper's attitude. He had been so nice before this and I was shocked he could change so quickly. Once the gardaí went in and said who I was and told him to sack me, he automatically forgot that he liked me. But I don't hold that against him – he didn't know what the police were like. Not many people do.

I grew up with that kind of attitude – of people who make judgments without looking past the lies. My dad taught me that night that we couldn't hold it against people, because they were the ones frightened of the police. It wasn't 'The General' the shopkeeper was scared of – it was the stigma of the gardaí coming into his shop, the need to be on the right side of the fence. To be associated with criminals and their families was too much. In their ignorance, people never bothered to look beyond that.

All the same, my father wouldn't allow me to let it pass and forget about it, and I'm glad he didn't – it was another lesson learned. I was in the right. I had to stand up for myself. I went back up to the shop that evening and gave the owner a right earful. I went on a half-hour rant about what a spineless, gutless puppet he was for sacking me. He shouldn't have tried to put me down because the police told him to. The shopkeeper just stood there with his mouth open. The gardaí must have warned him that there may be a backlash, and this was it – I was the backlash, me and my opinions. I left that shop with my head held high.

*

Around 1988, though, the fun and games were over. Things started to turn more sinister.

For example, the gardaí would smash into the back of our cars while we were out driving. One Christmas morning, the whole family was travelling down to visit my grandmother, our car stacked up with presents, when something rammed into the back of the car. It was the garda surveillance, and the car was speeding away from us in reverse. My father jumped out of our car and ran up the road after them, calling for them to stop. They called for back-up and he was arrested for dangerous driving.

The surveillance team surrounded the house day and night and each member of my family had their own bodyguard as such. A couple of detectives were to record the movements of the whole family, not just my father, and once the boredom got too much for them, they began to play little games, presumably to relieve the tedium of their long shifts.

Another disturbing event gave my family a good reason to be more vigilant when it came to keeping an eye on Phoenix Park's finest. Martin was out one summer evening in 1988 and we were all getting ready to settle down for the night. My boyfriend, Mark, had stayed quite late that night and we sat watching TV in my bedroom, which was situated at the back of the house. The high-beam searchlights shone on the ceiling and walls of the darkened room as we watched the movie, but we ignored it. Dad had gone out, but as usual a small posse of detectives sat on the back wall.

It was late when I heard the crash downstairs. We had dozed off watching the film and the searchlights were gone. The room took on a silent darkness. Mark sat up on the bed and said, 'What was that noise?'

'It's probably just me da coming back in,' I answered, lying back down on the bed, when we heard another bang downstairs. I switched on the lights. Moments later, the lights flickered and then went out.

'Get up and see, will ya?' Mark said. I rushed out the door. Halfway down the landing, I could smell fire.

I ran to the kitchen door and opened it. The heat from the flames, which by now were licking their way across the ceiling, was intense. I backed out quickly, screaming up for Mark, who by now was halfway down the stairs carrying my young sister and a cousin that was staying the night over his shoulders. My brothers, followed by my mother, came down and we all left the house. I could see the surveillance car parked across the road, moronic-looking grins spread across the detectives' faces. We called the fire brigade and then called my father. Within minutes my father pulled up outside the gate, followed by a slow-moving surveillance team, which stared at us from behind their masks. My father rushed over to us. We were all huddled outside, shivering with the cold and waiting for the fire brigade, our faces black from the smoke.

'Da, the kitchen is on fire. Martin and Chris are trying to put it out,' I spluttered, tears welling up in my eyes.

'Get them out!' he shouted as he ran in through the hall door, pulling off his mask.

The boys had succeeded in putting out the fire with a fire extinguisher we kept in the kitchen. Da went around opening all the windows. I could see him move from room to room, then he came out and told us to come back inside the house. He walked slowly up to the gate to close it. The garda escort rolled down his window. 'Pity you weren't in it, you cunt.'

Da ignored him and returned to the house. We called the fire station and told them the fire was out, but they insisted on coming out to make sure it was out and under control.

'You could have all been killed,' was the only thing my father said about that fire. He sat in his chair looking at us. We all stood in the sitting room, blowing thick black mucus into hankies, laughing nervously at each other's black faces. I stopped laughing and swallowed hard. I looked at my father as his eyes glazed over.

'You could have all been killed,' he repeated, slowly putting his hand to his mouth and squeezing his lower lip. His gaze began to follow the high-beam searchlight that burst in on the scene. The watching had resumed.

*

The gardaí assigned to the overt surveillance duty were beginning to show the effects of severe paranoia and, some would say, psychosis. They began to act very strangely. For instance, they looked at us as we walked to our car as a deranged person would look at their captors in a lunatic asylum, with strange little grins and inappropriate nodding of heads as we passed. The look of hate, of frustration, of 'we'll get you fuckers' crossing their faces as they pulled us over in the car for no reason whatsoever. In anger, they would rip the inside from the car door. All we could do was laugh at the escapade, with a serious note of 'You better fix that and leave the car the way it was' thrown in. This seemed to infuriate them further.

We took to cycling everywhere. My father decided that this was a good way to shake them off, plus there was the added bonus of getting fitter. He decided it would be best if we all cycled old-fashioned delivery boy bikes, so he scoured junk shops and antique fairs to find them. They weren't the easiest contraptions to cycle, but Martin would remind us that when these were originally on the road, cobblestones were the norm and told us how lucky we were to have the luxury of a smooth surface. We gave out about having to cycle at all, asking him why it was even necessary.

'We'll do it for the laugh,' he said.

'Ah feck it, I'll do it today, but I'm not doing it tomorrow,' I said. He kept it up for a few months, though, causing confusion to his surveillance team by making quick turns down one-way streets and pedestrianised parts of the city centre.

I gave up on the madness and went back to my car after the day when, while cycling out of Cowper Downs, already puffing with exertion, I felt the garda car pull up beside me. They came very close. I was busy concentrating on turning the pedals. I looked up and something caught my eye, something that took the strain out of my endeavour – all the occupants of the detective car wore Groucho Marx disguises, the plastic ones with the glasses and the moustache. I looked again, squinting in disbelief – a carload of Groucho Marx impersonators was trying to intimidate me, on my 1920s delivery boy bike! For a split second, I knew what it was like to be Martin Cahill. I pulled over to the footpath, shook my head and laughed. I walked back to the house, dropped my bike, got into my car and drove off.

Joking aside, many serious things began to happen. My mother would leave the house for the school run only to discover her car smashed up, windows all put in, tyres slashed. The petrol was always being siphoned from the cars. She would fill the tank that evening and the next morning it would be empty. The grinning face of one of the surveillance team greeted her on such mornings. She would completely ignore this little game of theirs and retreat to the garage, where a couple of gallons of petrol were stored. She didn't give a shit about the smashed windows – as long as the thing had petrol and moved and got the kids to school, she could deal with the windows later.

I knew there was something wrong one afternoon in 1988. I was in the front bedroom of our house in Cowper Downs and saw my father's car tear around the corner into the estate, followed closely by his garda escort. My mother was in the driver's seat and she had a look of terror across her face as she pulled up violently outside the front gate. Something was wrong. My heart was pounding as I rushed down the stairs and flung open the door to be confronted with my mother's agonised face. She rushed past me, followed closely my by father. I slammed the heavy hall door closed on the leering faces of the gardaí and followed my parents into the kitchen. My mother was hysterical and my father kept saying, 'Some fucking pervert has her.'

'No, they don't!' my mother wailed.

'You should have been there on time!' he roared.

The petrol had been siphoned from her car by the surveillance team and she'd had to go to her supply in the garage to refuel, which meant she'd showed up at the gates to Emma's school, St Louis in Rathmines, a few minutes later than usual. Her child, who was always at the gate, wasn't there. She never walked home alone – she wasn't allowed. She was only eight years old.

The teachers who were left said, 'She's gone home, someone has taken her home.' They called after my mother as she ran down the hall, 'She's okay, Mrs Cahill, she's gone home,' their voices rattling after her. My mother knew this was wrong; this was not what was supposed to be happening.

The guards pulled my mother over halfway up Rathmines Road. 'Name, address,' the usual bullshit. She blurted out what they wanted to hear, then sped off to where my father was to get help.

He panicked. He didn't know what to do. When she explained that she hadn't been there on time, he slapped her across the face. He had never raised a hand to her before, ever since they had met that day in the Buildings. The shock of this threw her into further hysterics. Never mind the slap, where was her child?

When they came to the house and I heard that my eight-year-old sister was gone, I ran out the door. Some instinct in me kicked in – **find her, find her**. Terrified, I ran out of the estate and up Cowper Road, past all the silent houses that hid behind heavy velvet drapes, houses that held secrets. Tears welled up in my eyes as I ran, looking for my sister. The surveillance car followed close behind me.

And unbelievably, there she was. Walking slowly towards me, a look of panic on her face, maybe just mirroring mine. I grabbed her by the shoulders. When I touched her, everything was okay again. Then the questions came.

'What happened? Where were you? Ma is going to kill you. Da is like a fucking madman. You better get in that house. Come on, for fuck's sake.'

My poor sister just kept shaking her head as my parents quizzed her as to what the hell had happened that day. It eventually came out.

Two men had met her at the gate with big smiles, saying, 'Emma, your ma sent us down to pick you up today.'

'I thought it was Da's friends,' she sobbed.

They dropped her to the top of Palmerston Road. 'Now walk home,' they said. She was only eight years old, she didn't know any better; she wasn't used to this shit. It was getting very serious now.

That night, my father single-handedly went out and slashed the tyres of hundreds of cars in the Cowper Downs locality. He even slashed the tyres of the surveillance team's cars as they snored in the night. The next day, the newspapers were euphoric in their deliverance of the news: HUNDREDS OF TYRES SLASHED ACROSS DUBLIN. THE GENERAL'S MEN HAD A BUSY NIGHT. They didn't know that he had done this alone. He said that a Stanley knife was the best tool for the job; a regular knife would have been useless.

'Da, how could you do this all by yourself?' I asked eagerly.

'It's only time, daughter, that's all. Time,' he smiled. I understood.

After my sister's abduction from her school, everything took on a more sinister note.

*

On Monday, 29 February 1988, he was released without charge after spending forty-eight hours in custody. He was questioned about attacks on cars in the south of the city that had happened after gardaí attacked my father's car outside Cowper Downs, slashing the tyres, smashing the windows and pouring battery acid over the bonnet. All of his associates' cars

were also attacked. This retaliation was the same as
that carried out during the 1970s in Rathmines after
the gardaí ran baton charges into Hollyfield and
battered everyone in sight. Then as now, you had to
hit back. The gardaí were forced to stop wrecking his
car and siphoning out petrol. While he was questioned, they took his clothes away. He sat naked for the
forty-eight hours, but he didn't mind. They wouldn't
give him back his clothes when he was being released,
but they threw him an old jumper and jeans. He made
a makeshift balaclava from the sleeve of the jumper
and went out of the station into the media spotlight.

*

'Martin! Martin, quick! They've done it, they're
planting something in the cistern. Get up here!' my
mother screamed frantically to my father, who was
downstairs, flanked by four Special Branch detectives,
sitting on the sofa with his head in his hands. He stood
up and the detectives moved in, blocking his way.

'Frances, what's going on up there? Watch them,
Frances, remember who it was. Get his name!' he
shouted up to her.

He began to laugh, a low, confident laugh. 'Yis
fuckin' eegits, yis can't even do that right,' he said.
Three of the detectives went up the stairs, the other
one staying downstairs with Martin.

I turned the corner into Cowper Downs, pushing
Luke along in a buggy. I began to run when I saw all

the squad cars and detectives surrounding the house, the blue flashing lights bouncing off the apartment block across the road. Something was up, there were too many of them. I pushed past the ban garda blocking the entrance to the house. I thought my father had been shot dead in the house. My heart was racing and I could feel the blood draining from my face. I left Luke in the hall in the buggy and pushed open the living room door. The relief to see my father sitting there with his hand up to his face was overwhelming. 'Da, what's wrong? What happened?'

The detective stood over at the fireplace and his face grew red as my father said, 'They planted a gun in the bathroom in the back of the toilet. Your ma caught them.'

I gave the detective a dirty look. He just looked away. 'Typical,' I said; nothing else came to mind.

Earlier on that evening, Martin was alone in the house when he saw detectives coming to the door. He thought that they were coming to arrest him and take him to Mountjoy because he hadn't signed the peace bond that he'd been ordered to sign by the District Court a couple of weeks previously. He covered his face with black shoe polish and put on a balaclava. He opened the door before they even knocked. He was quite surprised when they produced a warrant to search the house for firearms.

His suspicions grew immediately, so he asked them if he could search them before they entered the house.

They refused. He asked for a superior officer to be present for the search. They refused. The gardaí entered the house. Martin recognised them as part of the surveillance team that sat on the back wall. They scattered all over the house, each one going alone into different rooms, which was very unusual. When Martin was detained in the living room by two detectives, he knew they were up to something. He sat on the sofa and waited.

A short time later, Martin's wife and her two sisters arrived at the house. Martin shouted at them to go around the house and watch the gardaí to make sure they didn't take anything from the rooms. Frances ran up the stairs and went into the bathroom. When he heard her shouting down to him, he rushed past the detective keeping him downstairs and ran into the bathroom. A detective stood there, his face flushed a deep red, and he pulled a package from the cistern. Frances was shouting at the garda, 'I saw you put that there! I want your name! I saw you put it there!'

The garda asked Martin if he knew anything about the package. 'I'm taking no responsibility for that for that gun,' Martin replied.

'How do you know it's a gun?' the garda asked. The gun was wrapped tightly by black tape. It couldn't have been anything else.

'I'm taking no responsibility for that gun,' Martin repeated. 'My wife saw you plant it in the toilet.'

They told him to go downstairs and wait. The detective that planted the gun stood in the corner very quietly, looking embarrassed. He wouldn't give them his name. Martin began calling them 'thicks' and telling them that they'd messed up and couldn't do anything right. He sat there laughing behind his mask. They told everyone that they were being arrested for possession of a firearm. Martin was being taken to the Bridewell garda station.

'Listen, you go around and call Gareth Sheehan,' my dad told me. 'Tell him what they're up to and I'll be at the Bridewell.'

They arrested my parents and my mother's sisters, who were in the house at the time. The convoy of police cars tore out of the estate in a dramatic show. How were they going to talk their way out of this one? Heads would roll somewhere for being bloody caught sticking the gun in the cistern. Another detective had taken photographs as his colleague smiled and put the gun in. They nearly died when my mother walked in and caught the saps giggling like a couple of school kids up to no good. When they left, I tried to contact my father's solicitor but there was no answer to his phone. I decided to go around to his parents' house, who lived in a period mansion. I'm not sure why I went to them, but I was in a bit of a panic. His elderly father opened the door to me, and instead of turning me away and telling me to contact the solicitor at the office, he invited me into their hallway while he phoned his son and told him why I was there. He offered me a hot drink and told me his son would be there soon. I remember thanking him in my head and taking a huge, painful gulp of tea. The solicitor was soon down in the station, making complaints on my father's behalf.

They were questioned all night long. My father could stay awake all night chanting that he had nothing to say to them – that was his tactic to block out their voices. He told me that after chanting 'I have nothing to say to you' over and over again, he would start to go a bit bippy and he would have to concentrate on the words to get them out. He could be saying this for up to twenty-four hours without a break, so he had to be focused. That particular night, the shoe polish that was smeared over his face started to make him feel light-headed and a little woozy. The toxins in the polish were obviously affecting him, but he made it through the night. In the other cell, my mother just stared at the wall.

'We've got him now, Frances. Give him up, for fuck's sake – for your kids' sake!' the detective sneered, obviously just for something to say. He knew they had messed up. She didn't listen. She was gumming for a cigarette. She had brought them but had forgotten her lighter. One of the detectives kept blowing cigarette smoke into her face, but she kept saying to herself, 'I'm giving them up this time.'

Martin kept his chant up all night. He knew they had been caught planting the gun, so he didn't care what they said to him – he knew the law. He was walking in the morning.

The detectives questioning him told him that his friend Shavo Hogan had put the gun in the cistern when he'd been visiting Martin the previous Wednesday. They told him that Shavo had had somebody tip off the gardaí. They also said that Shavo and a detective had conspired to plant the gun before Shavo was sentenced, and it was because of this that Shavo got such a light sentence for possession of a firearm.

Martin knew this to be untrue, because he knew that when Shavo had been to the house on the Wednesday, he had been in Martin's company the whole time and hadn't visited the bathroom, and Martin showed him to the door, as he always did with everybody. The gardaí were trying to isolate Martin and turn him against his friends. But it didn't work.

The next morning, they were all released without charge. The posse of detectives that were on show the previous night were nowhere to be seen. The embarrassment had been too much for them. That was the end of the Tango Squad and the overt surveillance.

They'd been given their assignment by garda headquarters, who were convinced this method of intimidation would eventually make my father crack or slip up. They couldn't have been more wrong. He was far too clever for their mind games, which didn't affect him in the least. They followed him twenty-four hours a day; they tried to turn him against his friends; they wanted him to believe that one of his friends, Shavo Hogan, had planted the gun in his cistern in the bathroom at Cowper Downs and had given them a tip-off. He saw all this straight away. They couldn't get to him. Martin believed that the planting of the gun was a conspiracy to discredit friends or acquaintances of his. Their big mistake was using inexperienced gardaí. Some of these detectives were drafted from uniform rank gardaí and had probably never had to plant guns before. The Tango Squad thought they had it made by planting a police informant smack in the middle of Martin's life. He knew all about that too, right from the very beginning, and used it to his own advantage. The old cliché of keeping your friends close but your enemies even closer was what my father lived by. He knew everything about everyone who stepped foot in the door and many things about people who never came through the door.

I can honestly say there was absolutely no one like him. He was unique. He made those who knew him believe that he could do anything. That's why we found it so hard to believe that he was actually dead when he was shot. We really did believe that he was out there hiding somewhere, watching the whole thing and laughing. That was just the type of person he was.

*

The DPP decided not to press charges – presumably they didn't have enough evidence to get a conviction. They knew they were caught red handed this time. They would be hanging themselves if they tried to stick this on Martin, so they called it a day and made a retreat. They disappeared from the back wall, there one day and gone the next – but not quite gone; not quite.

When Martin was released from Spike Island prison in Cork after serving four months for refusing to be bound over to the peace, the surveillance team was disbanded. They had failed in their mission of putting Martin behind bars. None of their tactics to frame him or stitch him up had worked.

My father got us together and told us that even though they were gone from sight, they were still there. The covert surveillance had begun.

Sometimes I would see them, shadowy figures behind darkened windows, but we knew where they were so that was okay and my father played along, not really changing his routine and losing his tail when he needed to, so life went on. I think the neighbours were relieved when the police were no longer visible in the area. Peace at last. Now they could have friends over without the spectacle of the Irish police force pulling wheelies on their motorbikes outside Martin Cahill's house.

Chapter 7
Prison's Not Too Bad, as Long as the Spells Are Short

During the 1970s, crime in Ireland was rising. Armed robberies were being carried out. Most of the blame lay at the Provisional IRA's feet, but the rest lay firmly at my father's. In November 1974, he was charged with the robbery of a security van. The van had just loaded up at the Quinnsworth store in Rathfarnham when the gang struck. The charges were later dropped, as there was no evidence against Martin or his brother Eddie, who was also up on the charge. His brother-in-law, Hughie Delaney, who was also arrested in connection with the robbery, was later acquitted at the trial due to lack of evidence. They would retaliate against the gardaí for this.

In 1970, Martin received a four-year sentence over a suit.

Eddie had given him the suit and it was hanging on the back of the door when the police barged in. The owner's name was stitched on the inside of the bloody thing. Martin got four years for receiving stolen property. Everyone were shocked when he got four years – back in those days, you did four years for murder, but this was all part of the game. 'It was a shit-looking suit into the bargain,' Eddie recalled.

In 1975, his brothers Anthony and Michael, both only teenagers, were arrested on a murder charge. The murder charges against both of his brothers were dropped. There was no evidence for a conviction and, as usual, nothing came of the complaints against the police brutality. The same year, Martin was jailed for four years for possession of a stolen car.

This was not a good time for us. I was only six years old. We missed him terribly and our mother was lonely with just us to talk to. His friends never really came around while he was locked up, but his brothers would call and give our mother money to get by.

We visited him every week. We would pass through the visitors' waiting room in Mountjoy through to the visiting room itself, relieved to be free of the thick, dense cigarette smoke that hung in the air with no possible means of escape. Everything in this kip was locked in, even the air. The wardens, or screws, as they were called, looked huge. Everything was huge – the gates were huge, the bunches of keys were huge. I would run ahead over to the visiting room and see his face light up when he saw us. He'd stand up and give us hugs over the table. The screw would tap the table and my father would just smile at us. 'Don't mind him,' he'd wink at me.

When we left him there, my heart would sink and my mother's eyes would glaze over. She would just keep saying, 'See you next week, see you next week.' He didn't stop waving until we were gone.

He always had something for us, sweets from the prison shop or something he'd made us. He couldn't hand them over himself, but we could collect things at the gate on the way out. One time, he said he had a surprise for me. I picked up my package at the gate. I couldn't wait to get home to open it, so I opened it there and then. There were about twenty little dollies, all hand sewn by himself. They all had different coloured wool hair caught into two bunches, just like I used to wear my hair. This was a treasure. I thought about him sewing the dollies in prison and me imagining all the while that he was breaking rocks or something like that. I wasn't quite so scared of the prison visits after that; it wasn't as bad a place as I had imagined. Or at least that was what he wanted us to believe – he didn't want us to be afraid.

Martin just kept his head down and got on with things. But what the wardens didn't know was that he had a loaded gun hidden in his cell which he'd had smuggled into the prison. He never intended to use it – someone else had asked him to get it – but he also saw it as putting up two fingers to the prison service. He kept quiet, but inside he always felt one step ahead of them.

When he came out of prison in 1980, he seemed so much older. Even though we saw him every week, it made no difference. When he came home, it was very strange. Having him about the house was going to take some getting used to. I was very shy with him, like a stranger had moved in. This didn't last very long, though, and eventually things got back to normal.

We started to notice that the police were always around. If they weren't driving through Hollyfield Buildings, we were being raided or pulled over. Little did we know then that this was what life would be like until my father died.

*

I would say the 1970s were some of my father's best years. He and his young wife were happy raising the children together and he had his brothers and his parents close by. Martin's brothers John, Eddie, Anthony, Patrick (Padser), Michael (Stike) and little Gerard, who was a couple of years younger than me, were his life and he idolised all of them.

However, most of his brothers fell foul of the law and Anthony, John and Eddie were to receive long stretches in prison. Yet none of them were actually ever caught doing anything – they received long sentences for what were considered small crimes, though the brothers believed they were stitched up by the gardaí and framed. Either way, they were given stiff sentences, some handed down through the Special Criminal Court, a juryless court set up to try terrorist and subversive groups cases. Martin was always critical of the Special Criminal Court trying people

Frances with her father on her first communion day.

Frances and Martin with the children and Max in Hollyfield.

Frances's confirmation day in 1981. Christopher is in front.

Christopher's communion day in 1981.

Playing in the ruins of Hollyfield in 1979.

Martin (seated) on a family holiday to Courtown in 1986.

Top: Martin and Frances Snr. with Luke in Dublin Zoo in 1989.

Right: Martin outside court wearing his famous Mickey Mouse t-shirt in 1988.

Martin's 'One Flew Under the Cuckoo's Nest' stunt outside the
Four Courts in 1988.

Martin outside his pigeon loft in Cowper Downs.

Members of the surveillance team on the back wall and above the pigeon loft in Cowper Downs.

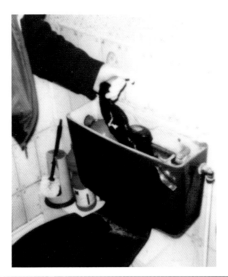

The gun being found in the cistern in Cowper Downs in 1988.

Martin and Luke in Cowper Downs in 1990, doing 'The General' (covering their faces).

The last family photograph: Martin holding his granddaughter Frances, with Frances (the author) holding her nephew, Christopher, two weeks before Martin was killed.

accused of a crime such as a robbery. He never believed such a system could be 100 per cent fair to the individual, as the SCC was not set up to try such crimes. Stiff sentences came with the territory. They got their time and did it. Prison was nothing to them – if the state thought for one minute that these institutions could break their spirits, they were badly mistaken. The battle with all authority carried on for them inside the jails. The screws were regarded as no better than the police, given that the screw usually came from a family with a garda in the bunch.

Anthony and John were each sentenced to ten years for their part in the Smurfit Paper Mills payroll robbery in 1978. The forensic evidence used against Anthony at his trial was overwhelming and there was no way out of it. Even though John was shot in the back by the guards while getting away on a motorbike, he still served the full term – no one in my family ever got a day less.

On 6 January 1982 Dr James Donovan, a forensic scientist, was the victim of a car bomb attack. Eddie has told me that Dr Donovan was a very unpopular man at this time and that the attack could have been carried out by any number of people – everyone was after him. Yet even though the paramilitaries were initially suspected and up to forty people were arrested and held for questioning, the blame for this attack eventually settled at my father's feet. No one has ever been convicted for the attack.

Eddie was released in May 1988 after serving a twelve-year sentence. Then, in November 1988, Eddie received an eight-year stretch in prison for being in the wrong place at the wrong time. He had gone to his friend Harry Melia's house to visit him. The police swooped and found some drugs on the premises. Eddie got eight years. It was yet another tag wrongfully and cruelly attached, but Eddie was used to it. If they can stitch you up, they will. You had to watch out for the traps, but he fell into one. The battle went on.

*

The planting of evidence to get a conviction was widely used, according to my father. 'To stop them planting the forensics, you have to watch everything very carefully,' he said.

My mother was under strict orders that if Martin was arrested or if anything should happen, she had to get all of his shoes and clothing into bags and get them out of the flat. This was because the police would raid it once they had Martin in some cell and gather what clothing or shoes they needed. These would then be sent off to the forensics lab.

On one occasion in the early 1980s, there was a burglary in a stately house in Wicklow. Footwear and clothing belonging to Martin were taken from the flat in Hollyfield by the gardaí. Fibres were then found on a pair of the shoes taken in the raid. The shoes, a pair of brown suede Hush Puppies, were brand new, bought a couple of days after the burglary in the house, but the receipt was nowhere to be found. I remember us all searching frantically for this receipt, with no luck. Martin was charged with the burglary and his trial went ahead. All the detectives who held grudges against Martin lined the gallery in the courtroom, smugly sitting, arms folded, waiting for the words 'guilty as charged'. This wasn't to be.

The woman who was at the house during the break-in said she heard loud footsteps of a man wearing hard shoes running across the wooden floor. The trial collapsed and my father was acquitted, as those soft Hush Puppy shoes would not under any circumstances make the sounds of the hard shoes that were described in evidence to the court. There was never any explanation as to how the fibres were found on the shoes.

After the acquittal, Martin made several protests outside the Dáil about garda corruption and the lengths to which certain people would go to get a conviction against my father. My two brothers and I gathered around him as he made his placards for his Dáil protest. We stuck cuddly toy puppy dogs onto the paper to represent the Hush Puppy shoes and the fibres which were found on them. He accused the government of being fully aware of this. His protest was against the lack of investigation regarding the Garda Síochána Complaints Board, which entailed police investigating police. This was as good as just throwing the complaint straight in the bin. He wanted to highlight that he could prove that there had been an attempt to get a conviction using evidence of fibres which could not possibly have been present on his shoes. It was as simple as that.

Over the span of thirty years of complaints about the gardaí, not one ever went anywhere.

*

During my father's spells behind bars, he always kept himself busy. He served an apprenticeship for a metalworker in Mountjoy, and for that reason he always liked Mark, my boyfriend at the time, who would later become my husband. 'He has a good trade. He'll always have a job,' he'd say.

He also learned to sew in Mountjoy, and needle-work became a favourite pastime for him inside. He was actually quite proud of his sewing skills – after doing his time in Mountjoy, he was always the one we went to if we needed a trouser leg taken up, a skirt hemmed or loose buttons fixed. He also took HGV driving lessons and passed the tests. He loved playing chess and taught most of the prisoners to play the game so he would have someone to go against. The boys in jail needed something to pass the time, and what could be better than something that exercised the mind? He was an expert chess player and was never beaten. The game gave you time to think; nothing was rushed, you could make your move when you felt like it and, as always, the main objective was to win. He was also behind the prisoners' rights organisation and fully supported all fights against miscarriages of justice, his attitude being, 'Let's all fight them together.'

While he was in Mountjoy prison, Martin presented an idea to the governor. Radios would be a good thing for the prisoners to have – it would take their minds off other things and they would be more relaxed if they had a little bit of music to listen to. Martin himself had a great love of music. The governor agreed to the idea and the prisoners in Mounyjoy got radios.

All he ever really said about prison was, 'It's not too bad, as long as the spells are short.'

*

My husband Mark's trade once took him inside Portlaoise Prison to carry out some specialist maintenance. The screws were offering the workmen tours of the wing which held some of Martin's friends and relatives. They told the men about the notorious Eddie Cahill, who was down in the basement (Eddie was kept in the base for years). The screws offered the workmen tours of what they called 'The General's Wing'. Some of the workmen went on the 'tour', but Mark declined, finding the whole thing bizarre and quite ridiculous.

*

The slashing of car tyres was another chapter in the ongoing battle with the gardaí. Everything was done for a reason, and this time, the police had vandalised my mother's car the previous day, slashing the tyres and smashing all the windows. When she came out of the house and found the car smashed up, the gardaí were sitting in their car, laughing at her. At the same time, in the prison where Martin's brother Eddie was serving time, the screws in riot gear were battering the inmates and making life hell. They didn't touch Eddie, though – he was too busy having his human rights breached by being placed in solitary confinement for years on end. His motto for life in prison was, 'Kill me or leave me alone.' They left him alone – literally. They put him down in the 'base' (basement) of Portlaoise Prison, where he served most of his time.

Martin and his imprisoned brothers felt that everybody on the outside knew of the abuses going on inside the jails and no one gave a shit. If screws were smashing in prisoners' heads, well, they had to keep them under control, didn't they?

While it seemed that ordinary, innocent people were suffering at the hands of the ruthless Martin Cahill, it was really retaliation towards the police and the prison authorities. And granted, it was also about giving people a little taste of what it was like to be on the receiving end of harassment and intimidation. Whenever the police did anything, Martin would hit back in this way, exactly the same way he had to hit back in Hollyfield. What was he supposed to do, sit back and take it? They should have known that if they hit him, he hit back even harder.

Chapter 8
I'm in the Jewellery Business

When Martin was robbing houses in the 1970s, he had an enormous amount of patience. He could watch and wait for days on end to choose his moment. He knew what to take and what houses to break into. He only robbed the wealthy ones – he never would have dreamed of taking anything from anybody who couldn't afford to be robbed. He believed the insurance companies could foot the bill – these companies were the big boys, robbing people blind, so let them pay something back.

Once he and Anthony followed a woman in her car back to her home. The flash and sparkle of her big diamond ring had caught Martin's eye. That night, they broke into the house, but they couldn't find the ring anywhere. Martin peeped into her bedroom and saw her lying asleep with the ring on her finger. He tried to gently ease the ring off without waking her up, but she sat up, startled, and Martin reassured her that all they wanted was the ring. She was obviously terrified to wake up to find two strange men in her bedroom, but he quickly put her at ease and she began to relax. After a while, Martin's brother made her a cup of tea and the woman began telling them how hard up she was and how that ring was all she had of any value. She started telling them which of her neighbours were worth robbing instead: 'Oh, such and such down the road has this and that.' She was a mine of information.

On another occasion, after breaking into a mansion on Palmerston Road, the occupants of the house, two gay middle-aged men, sat at the kitchen table with Martin and told them how skint they were. He sat between them with his balaclava on and listened to their domestic spat unfold.

'Now look here, we don't have any money for you to have. Look around you, we have nothing,' one of the men said.

His companion pursed his lips and said, 'Now tell him why we don't have any money.'

'Let's not have this discussion now, okay?' the first man replied, then looking at Martin said, 'We don't have anything, I'm afraid.'

'Oh yes,' the other one replied. 'We don't have any money because of you! You spend all the goddamn money,' he argued. 'We haven't even got the money to pay the electricity bill!' he growled at his companion. The argument continued for some time, and after several cups of tea, Martin left after giving them the money for the electricity bill.

These stories could easily portray my father as a modern-day Robin Hood figure, robbing the rich and giving to the poor. But there is no such thing as a good thief, only a person who steals either through desperation or because they've been given no other choice. My father was neither. He did what he wanted to do. He wasn't going to let anybody bring him down so low there was no way up. There was no way he was going to become a statistic of Ireland's depression, one of the faceless nobodies. They had robbed him of his chances in the navy and this was the only life left open to him. What was he supposed to do? Go down and stay down, frittering away the few bob he got on the dole down in the bookies? The gardaí would have loved that – it's where they want you, in your little box.

The truth is, I can't say what he robbed. I don't know exactly what he did or did not do. I can only talk about what I know and what I saw.

*

The progression to armed robbery happened almost by accident. When Anthony was about eighteen years old, he worked as a watchman near Dame Street. He had to just sit there watching the cars to make sure no one parked in the wrong place. Watching parking spaces all day was his day job – at night, he and Martin were breaking into houses. Anthony would see the security van pull up to the bank and unload the money. Then they brought more money back out to the van. He went home and told Martin what he saw, and Martin realised that he didn't need to rob the bank to gets its money, he just needed to rob the security vans. They were breaking into a house one night and found a gun, and that was it – they used that gun to rob security vans.

*

In 1981, Quintin Flynn LTD in Clondalkin, Dublin was robbed for the payroll. Martin and Christie Dutton, his close friend, were arrested and charged with the robbery. This was the one the gardaí were sure they could pin on Martin and get him behind bars for. During the trial, one of the vital witnesses for the prosecution said under oath that it was not Martin and Christie, that a pair of youths had held up the place. Martin had many arguments with his counsel during this trial – they weren't asking the questions that he wanted them to or stressing the points he wanted made. So he fired his counsel and represented himself for a while. His counsel came back to him after they informed him that they had something up their sleeve, but they had to wait for the prosecution to rest.

On 1 June 1984, Judge Martin instructed the jury to acquit both Martin and Christie due to a point of law. The witness was found not to have been in fear of her life during the robbery and so no crime had been committed. I arrived home that afternoon to find Dad sprawled out on the sofa, fast asleep. He was knackered after the trial. He was wearing a white jacket and white slacks with white shoes and a colourful tie. He was free. We were so relieved and happy. My father wasn't supposed to go to prison and he wasn't going down that day.

*

The Thomas O'Connor and Sons jewellery factory heist was to go down in history as one of my father's most daring achievements in his so-called criminal career. They say that he and members of 'The General's' gang emptied about €2.55 million worth of diamonds and gold from the factory in Harold's Cross in Dublin, leaving a bankrupt company and many unemployed people in its wake. Again, he would not have the privilege of being presumed innocent until proven guilty – in the gardaí's eyes, he and his gang had carried out the robbery.

After our school burned to the ground, Martin sent his children to the local Church of Ireland school, Kildare Place School in Rathmines. Most of the kids at this school were from the middle-class areas of Rathmines and Rathgar, so we made friends with the children of families that lived in the huge Georgian mansions that surrounded Hollyfield. One of my close friends at the school was the daughter of a District Court judge. After spending a lovely day at a birthday party at their beautiful home on Palmerston Road, her parents gathered all of the children into the huge hall to meet each parent as we were being collected. I could hear the roar of the Harley's engine as my father pulled into the gravel drive. My friends' parents were intrigued and quickly opened the front door. My father walked into the hall and introduced himself, standing there in his leather jacket with his motorbike helmet in his hand. 'A lovely house you have here,' he said, looking around.

The judge beamed. 'Mr Cahill, what a fantastic bike you're driving. Can I have a closer look?'

'Course you can. Do you drive? It's Martin, by the way. Call me Martin.'

The judge was very impressed with my father's bike and sat up on it. 'Goodness, it's heavy, isn't it?' he said. 'Are you in the music business, Martin?'

My father smiled at him. 'Ah no, no.'

'What is it you do?'

'I'm in the jewellery business,' he said, pulling on his helmet. 'Frances, say thank you for the party.' He handed me my helmet and I thanked them. They waved us off as he pulled off with a roar down Palmerston Road and towards Hollyfield. When we got home, I asked him why he had said he was in the jewellery business. 'I am, daughter. Sure, I'm into everything,' he laughed. 'Now let's see how fast you can run up them stairs.' I tore up the stone steps, with him chasing after me, the seagulls circling overhead and the law sitting outside.

*

The gang arrived at the place at the right time. Did everyone have their gloves on? Everything was set.

It was early morning and they were at the parking meter depot in Dublin. The plan was to tie up the female employee who opened the depot and make off with the money. Sure, it was a lot of coin, but what the fuck, it was money. He put his ear up against the door. He could hear something. He fell back when the door swung open. What the fuck?

Martin laughed as the scenario unfolded. They had come to rob the depot – and so had someone else, God love them. The hooded figures started to have an argument. 'What the fuck? Who the hell are you?' The whole scene was like something out of Monty Python, but it's a true story: two gangs had cased the place on the same night.

The argument went into full swing. 'We were here first, now get the fuck out of it!'

'No fuckin' way, we were here.'

'Jaysus, what's going on here? Who the fuck are they?'

'Me bollox!'

The two gangs sat on each side of the door arguing. Little did they know that the woman on the other side of the locked door was copping on pretty fast to what was happening. Martin decided she'd had too much time to get her thoughts together – the law would be on the scene soon. He made off shortly thereafter and the other gang followed. The woman won – she saved the coin that day. And spared the rest of the family, who would have had to count it.

*

The garda golf course at Stackstown, which belonged to the force and was used by high-ranking members of An Garda Síochána, was dug up one night in February 1988. Martin was accused of this in the media. The next day, after hearing that the course had had several holes dug into the greens, Martin said, 'Now they will definitely get a hole in one!' Although he never told me that he carried out this particular act, he loved this sort of thing. It would infuriate the guards, and anyway, he loathed golf, considering it an overindulgent, boring sport and a waste of lovely land.

*

'Hold still, hold fucking still!'

The biggest of the three pulled my arms around my back and quickly wrapped the black tape around my wrists. As he bit through the roll, he grunted at his accomplices to grab my feet. He threw the crude black tape to him and the other fella bound my ankles together. I took a deep breath and squinted my eyes closed tightly as one of them put a length of tape over my mouth. The biggest of the three grabbed me by the collar and pulled me close to his face.

'Now listen, you. Listen very carefully.'

Three weeks previously, the sun shone brightly as I happily carried my office equipment into my new office. I had signed the lease on a ground-floor room in number 74 Lower Leeson Street towards the end of 1992. I had collected my sign and was eagerly looking forward to hanging it on the door of my office. IRISH SACK SUPPLIERS. The sun filled the long Georgian hall as I screwed the sign to the white panelled door. Two girls who lived upstairs called out a cheery hello as they passed me. I nodded and smiled.

I had imported a container load of refuse sacks from a supplier in Malaysia. I began hawking them around the doors of housing estates with a little team of kids eager to earn some pocket money. Everyone bought them and after a few months I started to get orders from cinemas and restaurants. I hoped to eventually supply packaging to the retail and catering trade and was beginning to get a lot of contacts. My father was very proud of my effort and determination.

Now, the blood had stopped running to my hands and they were turning a deep purple colour. The black tape cut deep into my wrists. I noticed that the biggest fella's hands shook uncontrollably. As he pulled me in closer to him, I could see the sign on my office door, and even though I was in the middle of an attack from three men with black hoods pulled tightly over their faces, I was thinking of how proud I was of that sign.

Finally, the big fella spoke. 'Listen, you little bitch. You get the hell off this street and don't fucking return.

You get that bloody hot dog stand off those steps or we will come back and kick the shit out of you, do you understand?' He shook my collar and repeated the threat. 'Do you understand?'

I nodded in agreement, hoping they would just go. They left, walking out through the back door and into the lane behind the building. I was alone, bound and gagged on the floor of the hallway. I saw the sun shine through the glass of the large hall door and I relaxed in the quietness. It was over.

I thought I had better try to get some help. I began to kick on the wall and with a muffled cry tried to call out. At last, someone appeared at the top of the stairs. The girls who lived above must have heard my pathetic moans and came to investigate.

'Jesus Christ! What the hell?' The girl with a high-pitched Dublin 4 accent came down towards me and took the tape from my mouth. 'What happened? Who did this?'

'Please, just open the tape. Please cut the tape,' I replied.

She called out to her roommate, 'Bring a knife and call the police. Call the bloody police!'

As I sat in the garda station recounting what had happened (the girls upstairs had called them and taken me to the Fitzgibbon Street station), I had a feeling that the detectives weren't listening. They just stared at me with a puzzled look on their faces. I had given them my name. They didn't know what to say – I think they couldn't believe that I was actually making a report, being a Cahill and all. I left the station and headed home.

My father often spoke with a calm, quiet, reassuring tone and looked you straight in the eye. Sometimes this was a little unnerving, depending on the conversation, but today it was soothing.

'Explain every detail now. Don't leave anything out. Try to remember everything,' he said.

I told him everything that had happened that day – how I had showed up at the office in Leeson Street that morning, as usual. I opened the hall door and closed it behind me. I was fumbling with my keys, trying to find the key to my office door, when I was grabbed from behind. My attacker pulled me to the floor. I noticed there were three of them; I didn't stand a chance.

'Think, now. Tell me, what did they sound like? Did you recognise the voice?' my father asked, putting his arm around my shoulder.

'Yes, there was something. This was the first time – the big fella had never done anything like this. He was too nervous, the shaking of the hands, the tone of his voice, his mouth was dry. He seemed more scared than I was. And his accent, it was clipped' – what we called a yuppie accent compared to our Dublin tone.

Dad smiled and rubbed my head. 'Don't worry about it, daughter. Don't worry.'

That night, he went to Leeson Street.

A friend of my father's had begun selling hot dogs on Leeson Street. After being approached by a number of other hot dog sellers and local businessmen and told in no uncertain terms to take his business elsewhere, he approached my father with an offer of a percentage of the profits if he could persuade the other vendors that there was room for everyone. With his reputation, surely he would only have to show his face. This he did. However, certain people were so persistent with their threats that my father had to tell them straight out that his hot dog stand was staying.

By now, the gardaí had copped on to my father and promptly decided to try to end this little enterprising venture. Their intimidation began. They closed up all the stands, making it illegal to trade on the street. However, their powers ceased when the stands operated on the steps of the private dwellings instead, and the steps of my office became the ideal nocturnal retreat if you happened to be staggering out of one of the clubs at four in the morning, drunk and hungry. I believe business was good.

Shortly afterwards, the owner of my building, a small lady who wore a shabby fur around her shoulders, was told who I was. I'm sure once she heard who my father was, her mind was made up. She wanted me out.

She refused to accept my payments of rent and when I approached her, she brushed me off, saying that she wanted me out. I reminded her of our lease and her legal obligation to my tenancy (I'd only been there a few months at this stage). She turned to me and said, 'Get out of this building, Frances, and get out now.'

We ended up in court a few weeks later, me arguing that she had no right to terminate our lease and her arguing that I was allowing illegal activity to carry on at the front of her building. The judge ordered me to stop this from happening and I duly did.

The landlady took me to court again a few weeks after that to complain that I had broken that court order and that the hot dog stand was still trading from her steps. In my defence, I insisted that I was not giving anyone permission to trade from the front steps of the building. I told the judge that I had followed his instructions and advised my father's friend that it would be unwise for him to continue trading on the steps of this particular building, and he had agreed to move on.

The judge ordered a member of the gardaí to accompany me to the premises on Leeson Street to see if there was any evidence of illegal trading. We set off in the squad car, but I had to stop off home first to pick up the keys. Dad was in the sitting room, reading his paper. I quickly explained what was happening. He reassured me that I had done nothing wrong and I wasn't to worry about it. I took the policeman to the office. He poked around a bit. There was nothing there, no evidence to suggest I was trading at night, as indeed the vendor had stopped trading by then. Just as we were leaving to head back to the court, he picked up a cardboard box, looked inside and smiled. 'What's this, Frances?'

I looked in the box, which held bundles of paper napkins. It seemed that was enough for the judge. I was found to be in contempt of court and was sent off to Mountjoy.

My father was very angry – but not with the judge or the landlady. He was angry with me. After being in prison for about fifteen hours, I was allowed to make a phone call to my home. The priest in Mountjoy must have felt sorry for me. I had my mother on the phone and I was telling her how hungry I was. I had spent the night in the jail and the food – how can I put it? – the food would take some getting used to. I could hear my dad shouting in the background, 'Tell her to stop complaining. It's good experience. Tell her to cop on.'

I was released later that day. It was just a few days before Christmas, and rather than get high and mighty and refuse to apologise, I wanted to be home – there was no way I was going to spend Christmas in jail. (When you are found to be in contempt of court, you are sent to prison until you apologise to the court.) I apologised to the judge in the District Court, but the landlady's barrister tried to convince the judge that my apologies were insincere and that I was a member of an organised criminal gang, telling the judge it would be unwise to believe me. The judge nearly ran the barrister from the room, reprimanding him that he would not be told how to run his courtroom.

I immediately went back to the office at Leeson Street. I sat at my desk and began to sort through some papers when the door flung open, banging into the wall. The landlady, her husband and her twenty-year-old son stood in front of me. She clearly wore the trousers in her house. She looked like a menacing little pug dog as she pursed her thin lips together. Narrowing her eyes, she quietly growled at me, 'Get out of this building, Frances. Leave now.'

I refused. 'I'm not going anywhere. I am perfectly entitled to be here. I spent the night in Mountjoy and now that I'm here, I'll write you a cheque for any rent owed.'

I took out my chequebook and began to write. She lashed out and swiped the pen from my hand and pointed it into my face. 'Get the hell out of my building!' she bellowed.

Her husband and son moved in closer behind her, backing her up in a nervous sort of way. I knew that this was going to get serious. I grabbed the phone and called a friend. I told them to get up to my house and send my da down. As I hung up, the trio backed off. They all pulled up chairs and settled down to wait. Her husband constantly fidgeted in his chair, nervously watching the door, and her son began to pace up and down the room. The landlady just sat there, staring at the wall, furious that I had been released.

I began to talk. 'Why don't you just take the rent? Why are you giving yourself this hassle?' I asked. She stared blankly at the wall. I looked down at my papers and stated to tidy the desk a bit. I began again. 'You'll have to take me back to court to resolve thi—'

She cut me short. 'Oh no, Frances, **you** will have to take **me** to court next. We will let you face the costs this time.'

Before I could answer her, my eyes were drawn to a figure climbing through the open front window as the traffic on Leeson Street sped past. I was trying to pull all my thoughts together when I realised it was my father. I let out a sigh of relief.

The two men in the room quickly sat down and stared with wide eyes at this masked man, whose unconventional entrance had caused the blood to drain from their faces. Martin sat down quietly beside me. He rested his clasped hands on the desk and leaned forward towards the landlady, who didn't budge. Her expression didn't change, but I noticed beads of sweat quickly covered her top lip and her eyes started to flicker nervously as she stared at my father.

'Now what's wrong here?' he asked her.

I bit my lip to stop myself from laughing. She just

stared and a small smile crept across her face, trying to be brave, as he told her that she was only making her life harder, that all the unnecessary court costs were silly. Why didn't she just co-operate and let his daughter carry on her business?

She didn't answer and I was beginning to realise that she was starting to annoy him. He took off his mask. 'Now look at me, missus. I'm not the bad guy. The police have gotten to you and told you that I'm the big bad wolf. You should be smarter than that. Don't be listening to them. You leave this alone – she is paying you rent. Now you go home and take your family with you.'

With that, her husband began to speak. 'Yes, that's right, we don't want any trouble.'

The landlady put her hand in front of her husband's face without looking at him, scolding him to be quiet. He settled back into the chair and hunched his shoulders, giving my father a little nod as he exhaled loudly.

'I don't want you here. I don't want to rent this office to you,' she said without emotion and stared at my father, who at this stage was getting a bit fed up. He pulled his mask back on and gave a little laugh.

'Ah, daughter, you will have to deal with this yourself. I'll see you later,' he said, climbing out through the window. 'I'll come back later to check on you,' he said, looking back over his shoulder. He looked at the landlady again, shook his head and gave another little laugh, then he was gone.

It looked like it was going to be a long night and a battle of wits began. We were all prepared to sit this one out. After a few hours I realised it wasn't going anywhere. I felt sorry for her and her family and I left.

I was very upset when I got home. I was emotionally bruised by the experience I had just had. My father didn't say much when he saw me. He went through most of the rest of that evening sitting very quietly. Every now and again, he'd look in my direction and smile. I wondered what was going through his mind. Would he do anything?

That night before he left the house, he came over and said in a whisper, 'I'm gonna hang your woman upside down from her bedroom window.' He smiled.

I gave a little laugh. 'You are not...are you?' I raised my eyebrows and looked into his eyes to see if he was serious. He laughed as he walked towards the front door. 'Ah, no. Jaysus, she'd have a heart attack! See you later.' Then he was gone.

I stared out the window into the night and watched a huddled dark figure retreat from the garden wall, then heard a faint murmur and a crackle from the police walkie talkie radio. They were on the move again.

I never went back after that day. I left all my equipment. I was just sick of it.

*

At this time, Martin started to get serious threats from certain businessmen who made their livings from the dingy nightclubs that were housed in the basements of dilapidated Georgian houses in Leeson Street. This was before the property boom took off in this disintegrating area of old Dublin, when it was getting seedier and dirtier. He was told that certain businessmen on the street had connections with paramilitaries in the North and that they were going to have him killed – over a bloody hot dog! This was supposed to frighten him off, but he only found these threats insulting and told them there was room for everyone on the street, but no room for people who thought they could bully him with ridiculous IRA threats. He was used to that crap.

One of the clubs went up in flames and another small, dingy restaurant had a kitchen fire. My father was connected to these fires in the press. A local businessman who ran a grimy bistro on the Leeson Street strip, Wolfgang ('Wolfie') Eulitz, was supposed to have got shot in the leg by a person in his flat at the time of the fires in Leeson Street, and he allegedly believed my father had been responsible for the shooting. However, Martin was producing his driver's licence in the Rathmines garda station at the time of the incident involving Wolfie, so this would have made it physically impossible for him to have carried out this act. (Martin often produced his licence at the garda station.)

During an interview on the 2FM **Gerry Ryan Show** in 2006, both the presenter and Wolfie sounded ridiculous, with their accusations and unfounded remarks, all these years later. Even when there was proof that Martin Cahill could not possibly have carried out an act, he was still handed the blame. But it didn't matter. 'Let them say what they want,' he'd say. 'What real harm can they do?'

It means nothing whatsoever to us as a family to hear all sorts of allegations and lies about my father. One of Martin's favourite expressions was 'like water off a duck's back'. This is exactly how we feel about people making ridiculous accusations about Martin. My family has chosen to ignore outlandish accusations from people eager to make names for themselves. As my father would have said, **que sera, sera**.

*

I don't know anything about the Russborough House robbery that hasn't been said in the press before. Martin never talked to me about it. What I do know is that the paintings stolen from Russborough House in May 1986 were a thorn in the gardaí's side. It's a familiar story by now: a gang of thieves led by my father under cover of darkness managed to break into the house and steal twelve of the paintings from the Beit Collection, worth £30 million altogether, one of the most valuable being **A Lady Writing a Letter** by Vermeer. The police were then shamed worldwide over the fiasco of trying to recover the stolen paintings, and the embarrassment was to stay with all involved for the remainder of certain high-ranking members of the police force's professional lives.

The thieves cut a small pane of glass out of a window and entered the house to trip the alarm. They then retreated and hid in the bushes, until the gardaí had come and gone, believing it was a false alarm. An hour later, the thieves went back inside and took the paintings from the walls.

The gang that stole the Beit Collection was well aware of the nearly impossible task of selling it, as the paintings were too well known. The Beit Collection was stolen to send a strong message to the people Martin called 'the golden circle'. These were the really rich, the wealthy elite. They believed they were untouchable. They believed the gardaí would take care of them, that the gardaí would look after these hoodlums, as they called Cahill and his 'gang'. They were wrong.

Sir Alfred Beit belonged to this 'golden circle' and was the first target. Sir Alfred was a good friend of the Irish media tycoon Tony O'Reilly, and now that the newspapers were beginning to tell their demonising stories about Martin and his brothers on the gossip pages, this so-called 'golden circle' became part of the battle, joining the list of Martin's enemies. Sir Alfred had his paintings stolen for the simple reason to prove that these people were not untouchable. It also made the gardaí look incredibly stupid. It was all part of the game. The paintings were never taken for their value, but what Martin got from the robbery was very valuable in his eyes: he sent out a message that went straight to the point.

He was sick of these people thinking that they could say what they wanted and siding with the police. That was their mistake – siding with the police. He didn't care what anyone ever said about him – you could call him a bollox for all he cared – but never side with the police.

There is a theory out there that Martin stole the paintings and sold them to the Ulster Volunteer Force, which is what sealed his fate with the IRA. I don't know what happened to the paintings or what my father's involvement would have been. All I can say is that Martin didn't have any allegiance to anybody and had no loyalties to any paramilitary organisation on either side of the Troubles. He would have sold the paintings to whoever bought them; it wouldn't have mattered to him who he sold things on to.

In any case, Martin never had any interest in robbing the paintings for money. He did it because he wanted the boys in the Park to know he was going after the real money now. He was hitting them where it hurt. These people didn't care about money – they had enough of that; he was going after their trophies. In Sir Alfred's case, it was his prized paintings.

*

When the Beit Collection was stolen from Russbourough House, all hell broke loose when the gardaí in police headquarters came to the conclusion that Martin Cahill was the culprit, ruling out any paramilitary involvement. (In 1974, an armed gang stole nineteen paintings from Russborough House worth £8 million, demanding the return of Irish republican prisoners from England as well as a £500,000 ransom. British heiress Rose Dugdale was later convicted and sentenced to eighteen years in prison for the theft of the paintings, as well as an earlier IRA operation. It thus looked like a job the paramilitaries wouldn't touch with a barge pole.) It was believed Martin had decided to move into a more high-brow occupation as an art thief. Our family's previous visits to Russbourough could now be seen as Martin's easy casing of the job.

Not that we as a family would have noticed on the day. The picnic we enjoyed on the lawn at Russbourough is a memory I shall always treasure.

We had a family outing to Russborough House one afternoon about six months before the robbery. We walked around the gallery as Martin explained each painting to us in detail. We got a little bored and left him alone in the room, staring at the paintings. His favourites were the Vermeer and Francisco de Goya's **Portrait of Antonia Zárate**. He thought the woman in this painting, the beautiful actress Dona Antonia Zárate, looked sad but extremely beautiful. 'She looks like my mother,' he said and smiled.

Mother had brought a picnic in the huge picnic basket my father had bought her. She lay with her head in his lap, sipping wine, and he leaned back on the grass, wearing his panama hat and admiring the magnificent Palladian mansion. Dad was so relaxed and happy. We could have been any family relaxing on the lawn.

Contrary to the popular belief that Martin was illiterate, he was far from it – he was an avid reader. He also loved art and we had many books on the subject in our house in Cowper Downs. Sometimes he would visit the National Gallery of Ireland, the police right on his tail. He would pull up across from the gallery, park his car and saunter in. The police would surround him, taunting him as he stood there, just staring at a painting for up to an hour. This drove the gardaí crazy. He knew he was really annoying them by visiting the gallery, but he also genuinely enjoyed the art.

As a boy, he would visit the gallery and stare for hours on end at the works of art – until the staff would show him the door. Galleries in those days didn't favour the working class, and a child by himself must have been up to no good. He would tell me about the art he loved. His favourites were the Old Masters, in particular a Renoir that was hanging unpretentiously in a dark corner of the gallery.

Over time, all but two of the paintings were found, most in Britain and Belgium, and shortly before my father's death one of the last important pieces was recovered. Sir Alfred had nothing to fear now if Martin Cahill was killed, as the risk of his paintings forever lying in some bunker somewhere was not a possibility any more.

Even though there was no evidence to link my father with this robbery, he will go down in Irish history as the person who stole the famous collection. But as always, his reasons were very simple – if you hit us, we will hit back even harder.

*

'I'm watching them, Martin, I'm watching them from the fuckin' playhouse in the fuckin' garden.' He threw back his head and laughed, then looked at my father, searching his face for a sign that my father thought this was a good idea. Martin didn't smile. He didn't say anything.

Of all the people my father was associated with in his relatively short life, this guy was one of the most dangerous and sinister. This man, a fella my father saw on and off, was plotting to kidnap Bono and Ali Hewson's eldest daughter. He had placed a team of five men to case the house in Killiney. For six months they knew Ali Hewson's every move and the children's routine, from school pick-ups to music lessons. Every now and again Bono would appear on the scene, but mainly it was the mother, children, friends and staff who were under the constant gaze of a man whose only motive was the thought that a monetary figure in the region of £6 million was to be had. Every move the family made was documented every day for six months, even down to the food they had in the cupboard – every last detail had been recorded.

All they needed now was for Martin to come on board. With him in charge, the plan would be foolproof.

These people were amazed at how vulnerable the rich allow themselves to be. When he was in a reflective mood, my father would tell us, 'If you have something of value, there is always someone out there who wants it,' adding, 'never leave your bedroom curtains open – there is always someone watching.' He had this way of always putting you on your guard. And the Hewsons should have been on their guard.

He told them it was a bad idea. This didn't rest easy with the people who had painstakingly cased the target for half a year.

'This is it! Martin, I'm telling you, this is **it**!' the man said.

Martin had nothing against Bono's family. They had never done him any harm and he wasn't going to get involved. He leaned forward into the conversation. 'Now listen, will ya? This is not gonna happen. Are you listening? Now listen to me. This is not gonna happen for the simple reason it is not going to work. Not where the kids are involved. It's too much. I won't have anything to do with this.'

The atmosphere in the sitting room was heavy; cigarette smoke hung in the air. The guy knew Martin meant what he said. He pulled deeply on his cigarette and exhaled. 'What about his aul' fella then?' he smiled, and the room erupted into laughter.

Martin stopped laughing and leaned in closer, almost whispering, 'Well, tell me what's happening so far.'

The kidnapping plan around Bono's family went nowhere. The person who made the initial plans had been deterred by Martin and, unknown to themselves, the Hewson family was spared the terror of such an ordeal.

*

The kidnapping of wealthy businesspeople and their families was to become something of a phenomenon in Ireland. My father recalled how a gang was planning to kidnap Norma Smurfit of the Smurfit dynasty, one of the wealthiest families in Ireland, but changed their minds when, on the evening of the kidnapping, Mrs Smurfit, sitting in her kitchen doing embroidery, looked so peaceful and content doing her needlework that she cut a sort of melancholy figure and it was decided to abort the plan. They felt sorry for her and the gang went home and that was that. Norma Smurfit could finish her embroidery.

The kidnapping of the National Irish Bank chief executive, Jim Lacey, and his family in 1993 was to catapult my father into a whole new arena. This sort of crime was extremely hard for the gardaí to deter, and with Martin Cahill supposedly at the helm of this particular method of crime, no one was safe – or so they said.

The banks had begun to annoy Martin. They had started giving out information to the gardaí – confidential information. He had never held a bank account, but my mother's accounts were being infiltrated by the gardaí, thanks to the bank. She never even had that much money in an account – it was the principle behind it that upset him. He hated anyone who helped the gardaí.

The man the kidnapping gang had on the inside was alleged to have been a senior executive at the National Irish Bank (make no mistake, there is always a man on the inside). He was to give the gang details of a secret room holding cash, and this bank in particular had a lot of hidden money – about €8 million. He supplied details of all executives who had to be cased for what their role was and what pull they had.

Almost immediately after the kidnapping, when the papers got a whiff that Martin Cahill was involved, he was automatically considered to be the culprit –

never mind the fact that he'd been at my engagement party that night. Another trial by media took place, reminiscent of that kicked off by the **Today Tonight** programme in 1988.

For Lacey, the robbery was a spark that eventually turned into a flame that would not only taint him professionally, but would uncover one of the biggest banking scandals in Irish history. An internal audit carried out in 1994 after the robbery uncovered one of the worst tax evasion scandals the country had ever seen. The investigation discovered that 40 per cent of non-residential account declarations were missing or incomplete, which was ignored by the bank's senior executives. This was to end the high-flying career of not just Lacey, but many senior executives at the bank. The scandal prompted investigations into all the major banks and the Exchequer recovered billions in revenue for the country. Due to the investigations, Mr Lacey had plenty of reasons to curse the person who held his family for ransom that cold November night.

On 1 November 1993, Jim Lacey, CEO of the National Irish Bank, was held captive by a gang demanding that Mr Lacey was to go to his branch and take money from the vaults. He was to be accompanied by another man who was also being held captive by the gang. The rest of the Lacey family – Mrs Joan Lacey, their four children and a babysitter – were moved from the house and held elsewhere.

The following morning, Jim Lacey, accompanied by the other kidnap victim, drove to the branch in Dublin. Lacey told colleagues at the bank that his family were being held and that he was under instructions to fill up the hold-alls he'd been given by the gang. After some discussion amongst his colleagues, the banking executive put the money into the sacks and the other man, later named as Joseph Kavanagh, loaded the sacks into the van and drove off with the cash. Mr Lacey and his colleagues then went against their direct instructions from the gang to wait until an appointed time to call the police and called the gardaí in early – even though Lacey's family was still being held. However, the Lacey family were released later that day, unhurt.

The day after the kidnapping, my father lay stretched out on the sofa surrounded by his news-papers. He smiled as I entered the room. 'Hello, daughter, what's up?'

'Da, you know they're saying it's you who did that kidnapping last night, don't you?' I looked at him, hoping he would at least get a little angry. He just smiled.

'These damn papers, Da – you have to do something about them.' I was getting angry. I was sick of the accusations.

'Let them say what they want. I'm keeping it all up here,' he said, tapping his head. 'Jaysus, I believe Mrs

Lacey fought like a man,' he said, straightening out the newspaper and disappearing behind it.

*

On his release by the gang, Joseph Kavanagh went to the gardaí and reported what he had been through. He was later arrested and charged with his 'part' in the kidnapping and the robbery. He was tried before the Special Criminal Court and subsequently found guilty and sentenced to two terms of twelve years and one term of five years, all running from July 1994. His appeal was dismissed. Kavanagh argued that it was unfair to hold his trial in the non-jury court which was established to deal with trials with a subversive or a paramilitary connection.

In 2001 a landmark ruling by the United Nations Human Rights Committee found that Kavanagh should not have been tried in the Special Criminal Court without a specific reason being given. The state was 'also under an obligation to ensure that similar violations do not occur in the future; it should ensure that persons are not tried before the Special Criminal Court unless reasonable and objective criteria for the decision are provided.' Kavanagh's lawyers called for his conviction for the kidnapping to be quashed and for his immediate release.

*

I think the Jim Lacey kidnapping was Martin's undoing and was a catalyst for his murder. Lacey was too well connected and it sent shockwaves right through the upper echelon of Irish society, that 'golden circle'. 'The General' had gone too far this time.

Chapter 9
The Man behind the Mask

I suppose I realised my father was different from other fathers when he would open large sacks of money. 'Now you stack the pound notes and count the fivers,' he would instruct, 'and you count out all the twenties and you count out all the fifties,' my brothers were told. We would sit wide eyed at the stacks of cash, then pounce on our little numerical assignments. The amount of money was beyond comprehension to our young minds. We were about eight or nine years of age, sorting out bundles and bundles of money – thousands of pounds – each into neat little piles. Most of the money came from tight bundles of black plastic wrap. Counting money or sorting out money was just a way of life. Sometimes notes would be hung out to dry on the washing lines – money that got wet had to be dried, after all. It was only when I got older that I looked back and realised this wasn't exactly normal, but as a child I didn't question it.

I remember playing one afternoon with my friend at the drying yard in Hollyfield. She unearthed a large sack and opened it with relish while I sat back, suspicious. She held up bundles of cash in each of her little fists and laughed. I didn't laugh; I knew better. I ran home and told my father. A few hours later, we were back out playing. She was twenty pounds richer. I got a pat on the head and a smile.

Another time, when I was around ten years old, I walked into the flat to find a couple of men there, waiting for Martin. I thought one of them had a small handgun and he was rubbing an oily black rag over the barrel.

'How are ye, Frances?' he called as he saw me come in and put the gun in a bag.

'Where's me da?' I asked.

'He's coming now, you go on out and play. Here's a few bob,' he said and handed me a fiver. That was the only time I ever saw a gun until, years later, I was walking down Rathmines and, passing the Bank of Ireland, I noticed a couple of ladies climbing out a small side window, their skirts pulled up high. Once out, they ran towards the footpath.

'Quick, call the police,' one of the women quietly mouthed to me. She looked terrified and the other woman was in tears. I realised the place was being held up. The next thing I knew, the robbers were running from the entrance of the bank. Seeing them, one of whom held a small shotgun down low, the men at a nearby bus stop dove for cover in a shop. I froze and waited for them to pass me. I nearly died when the last of the raiders running from the building ran past me and said, 'All right Fran?'

What the hell! I thought. Who the hell was that?

That was the closest I had come to crime in my whole life.

*

My father was many things to many people. We constantly had callers to the house. Depending on who came that day, his role could be marriage counsellor, banker, friend, or just somebody to tell your troubles to if a neighbour was fucking about with the wife.

All the visitors to the house made everyday life...well, let's just say you had to open the door a lot. It was slightly irritating, to say the least, but we didn't really mind. It was just a normal day for us.

Martin really should have had an appointment system in place due to the number of people who came to our house every day. These people would come for advice, for help, for a lend, for a friendly, under-standing chat. I swear, if he had charged he would have made a fortune. Much talking and many cups of tea later, he would always show them to the door. Sometimes he had other people waiting in the hall to see him while he was with the other person, giving advice or whatever it was.

He gave away loads of money as bail money, or to friends who had a business idea, often never seeing a penny of it back. I had a friend who got a £15,000 loan off him, but her business wasn't going well and she couldn't pay it back. When she told him, he just said to bring him two bags of pigeon corn every week and that would be enough. Come to think of it, a lot of people repaid him in bird seed. My friend's brother was into bikes and asked Martin if he could have a lend of one of the bikes to have a spin up at the Dodder. I saw him later that day and his face was white – he'd crashed it. When he told Martin, Martin was so disgusted he just walked away and didn't say anything. My friend's brother later told me he wanted to pay for the damage, but Martin said to just give him a bag of seed every week. So every week, a bag of seed would be thrown in the back garden; he wouldn't even come in. That gesture was enough for Martin to know he was truly repentant.

*

Many people came to see if he could get them out of their troubles and give them money, which he often did, much to my annoyance. My mother never seemed to mind who he would give his last penny to. I was slightly more suspicious of their motives.

One time, when I was about fourteen, I went into the living room to find my father sitting in his usual chair by the open fire. On the other side of the room, on the sofa, sat a very large lady of about fifty. She was sobbing into a handkerchief and blowing her nose forcefully. My dad looked over to me and put his finger to his mouth, shushing me into silence. I sat down, pretending to watch television, one ear cocked to hear her story. This should be good, I thought to myself.

She spoke in a whispered voice, eyeing me suspiciously as she continued with the conversation. I could see she would have preferred if I got the hell out, but I stayed. My da would never tell me to leave.

'What'll I do, Martin?' she muttered into the soggy hanky. 'Jaysus, he's a bollox.'

'Most of them are, Breda,' my father replied. The woman's sobs grew louder and my da looked at me. 'Fran, make a drop of tea, will ya?'

I went to the kitchen and made the tea. The conversation continued once I left the room. When I walked back in, she sobbed once more into the hanky, which was now just a mass of small wet scraps in her rough hands. I handed her the cup and she looked up from the hanky, her face wet with tears. I nearly dropped the tea when I saw the state of her face. Her two eyes were black and swollen and her top lip was bulging out over the lower lip. Dried blood was caked into the corners of her mouth.

'Thanks, love,' she whispered. 'She's a lovely girl, Martin,' she smiled.

My father took her hand and smiled at her. 'Now you don't be worrying about anything, do you hear me?' he reassured her, then moved in closer. 'Where did you move the gun?' he whispered.

He looked over to me again. 'Fran, get a few biscuits or something, will ye?'

I left the room but could still hear Breda sobbing from the kitchen as I tried to listen.

'Martin, he took it. He moved it, that bollox, he took it. Help us, will ye, for God's sake.' Breda was getting too loud; the bugging devices would pick her up.

'Stop now, stop it, okay? Don't worry about it,' Martin shushed her.

I came in with the biscuits and Breda smiled at me as I handed her the plate. 'Ah Martin, she's gorgeous.' I could feel my face going red.

'Don't mind her. She knows it as well.' He handed her a handkerchief and she blew her nose into it with a loud snort. I looked over at my father and he raised his eyebrows and smiled at me.

Martin had given Breda's husband a package a few days earlier and told him to hide it. And he did, of course – he would do anything for Martin Cahill, no questions asked. Breda found the package and, thinking it was her husband's, she hid it on him and wouldn't tell him where it was, so he had kicked her up and down the stairs of their house. Even after he battered her, she wouldn't give in. Martin got his package back after he used his soft approach with her, always the charmer.

My mother would jokingly call him forty face. 'Ah, you have to be forty faced,' would be his reply.

*

'Whatever you do, right – are you listening?' My father looked at me with a smile sneaking onto his face. 'When you're walking home late at night—'

'But I'm never in that situation,' I interrupted, trying to look convincing in a wide-eyed, innocent sort of way.

'Right, right, just let's say you're walking home alone late at night on your own,' he replied with a hint of frustration in his voice. 'The street is quiet. You're trying not to run. You're walking as fast as you can, trying not to panic. You're starting to sweat as you start to walk a little quicker. You keep looking over your shoulder.' He smiled as I nodded knowingly. 'Now you feel the danger. You can't see anyone, but you can feel the danger lurking. You can feel someone watching you, right?'

'Yeah,' I said slowly. 'Now what?'

'Don't do it, okay?' he said, lowering his head and looking at me like a headmaster would over the rim of his glasses. 'Don't bloody do it,' he sang. 'Go through the gardens, crawl over bushes – whatever you do, don't walk down that road.'

'Ah, Da, would ye go away, you're mad! Imagine me crawling through gardens and climbing over walls to get home! You're mental. Anyway, I'd probably bump into a murderer in one of the bloody gardens.'

'Well I'm telling you, he is going to be more afraid of you than you are of him,' he chuckled, then disappeared behind the newspaper he was reading.

He was always giving advice, always telling you what was what, and his advice was always taken on board, stored in the back of your mind. You never knew when you might need it. Most people who had close contact with my father came to him for advice and for help at one time or another. Women and men from all walks of life would regularly visit the house in Cowper Downs to have a chat. The doorbell would ring five, six, seven times a day.

'How are ye, is yer da there?' they'd say, or if it was someone we knew, 'Is he in?' We would go to my father and whisper, 'Are you in, Da, it's so and so.' Depending on who it was and whether he was too tired or not, we would more often than not show the person into the living room or out into the garden if he was busy with his pigeons.

Cups of tea usually followed as you were given a warm welcome and an equally warm smile from him. One of my father's most appealing qualities was his ability to make you feel important. He always sat up and leaned forward, listening intently to what you had to say. He would have this look of concentration on his face – he did something with his mouth, not pursing his lips, but pulling in the lower lip so his top lip sat over the bottom. He totally concentrated on the conversation and never butted in, but really listened, engrossed.

Many of the people who passed through our various living rooms over the years to have a word with Martin didn't really know him. Many just came because he had the reputation of a man who could sort things out for you: 'Ah, go up to Martin, he'll help us' or 'Go up to Martin Cahill, he'll put the bail money up' or 'Get Martin down here, he'll sort them out'. The funny thing was, he could help and he did most of the time. He never went around beating people up or anything like that – he didn't have to. He hated bullies and would always avoid any sort of violence. All he usually had to do was show up and give the person a warning. He would be very diplomatic in his approach, always calm and quiet. His warnings were subtle. He could say something like, 'I'll give you one hour to do what I want you to do and then I'll come back.' He would go up close to the person and say, 'Look at me. I'm warning you – I will come back.' He found wearing his balaclava mask to be very effective. It was usually enough to scare someone, though if he was genuinely annoyed he could look quite menacing, sometimes going into a rage, but he never lost control.

*

My father had many acquaintances, but only a small few he would call his friends, and he held those few close men in very high regard. There was Eamon 'Eamo' Daly, a very old and loyal friend to my father. Eamo came from a middle-class background and met my father in the 1970s. Eamo was a quiet bloke with a kind face. He was in and out of prison most of his life, but when he was out he was a close companion to my father. Then there was John Foy, my dad's brother-in-law, and close friend Eugene Scallon, another brother-in-law.

In his circle of friends, Martin was by no means the boss, despite what his nickname might imply. Some of Martin's friends called him 'Arthur' (Arthur came from the name Martin, as in 'Mart' or 'Art'). Then some people called him 'Mac', which went on to be 'MacArthur'. One night, while amongst a group of friends in Hollyfield, his brother-in-law, Hughie Delaney, after being asked by Martin to do something, stood up and joked, 'Okay, General MacArthur.' The name stuck. But no one ever called him that – the tabloids, fuelled by the gardaí, latched on to the alias. The nickname was perfect for being able to accuse 'The General' of crimes while still circumventing the libel laws.

They were all equal, there was no ringleader. The inner circle was very close and knew they could trust each other. They all grew up together and Christy was the only one who wasn't related to the others. Outside of this group of friends there were a lot of hangers-on, men with dubious allegiances, often informers or drug pushers. Most of the inner circle didn't like the hangers-on, and didn't like the influence they had over younger, more naïve people. The hangers-on would use their association with Martin to impress these young men and get them involved in activities such as drug dealing, something Martin would never be involved with himself. His close friends did not want him to continue to associate with the hangers-on, but Martin followed the theory that you should keep a close eye on your enemies.

*

Another part of Martin's character was his ability to surprise. For instance, he didn't always appear in public or in court in his usual attire of balaclava and anorak. When he appeared on an appeal against a £70 fine for careless driving, he surprised the packed courtroom when he showed up in a smart blazer and perfectly pressed trousers with a white shirt and a red and black tie. He had discarded his famous balaclava and he didn't cover his face at all. The gardaí that lined the courtroom wall all stared hard at him – most had never seen his face before. His appeal was upheld. When the state solicitor attempted to protest the decision, Judge Hanrahan told him to sit down. Martin told waiting reporters that he was pleased with the decision, saying, 'I'm always a careful driver and I don't drive dangerously. You can rest assured that I will be very careful in the future and will always be wearing my seat belt.'

*

Martin would talk for hours over the dinner table and discuss cases involving corrupt judges and politicians. He would go on about the gun-running Charlie

Haughey, calling him a 'corrupt bollox', and how the gun used to kill Garda Richard Fallon during a bank robbery was one of the consignment of firearms smuggled into the country by Haughey for para-militaries. He said he was watching the then Minister for Finance, Bertie Ahern, very closely. He predicted that Ahern would follow in Haughey's footsteps one day, in more ways than one.

Martin would sometimes pick a politician to target – once he had them in his sights, he would, in his words, 'track them', or watch them closely, keeping an eye on where they went and who they met outside office hours, his reason being that the information he gathered on people could come in useful one day. He had the lowdown on every senior politician in Dublin. He would sometimes have a snoop around their houses or Dublin apartments when they weren't there. It was almost a hobby, something he enjoyed.

He would describe Ahern as a sly dog, one of the most devious politicians since Haughey. He would have roared with laughter if he had been alive to hear Ahern tell a shocked Dáil assembly in 2006 that between 1987 and 1994, when he was Finance minister, he didn't have a bank account. Martin said, 'These people don't take their money into the bank through the front door, it's always through the back door. Me, I'll take it out through a hole in the roof.'

*

Martin had many collections. For instance, he had a huge collection of coins, his favourite being a gold commemorative Eamonn de Valera coin. He hid this collection behind the skirting boards in each house we lived in, as he knew that if the police got their hands on them, he would never see them again. He would take them out to polish and admire and show them to us, explaining what each coin was and where it was from.

He had a large collection of 1920s delivery boy bikes and would buy my mother novelty teapots – she had around 150 teapots in the house. She wasn't really a collector, but he loved to collect things. He also had old-fashioned objects like an old wrought iron plough, which he kept in the front garden in Cowper Downs, and old kettles that were used on the fire.

He also had a collection of Disney memorabilia, like plates and figurines. His favourite was a porcelain music box of Mickey and Minnie Mouse sitting in a car that played 'You Are My Sunshine'. He would wind it up any time he'd come into the room where he kept it, grab my mother and twirl her around the room to the music.

Other than his passion for motorcycles and his collections, Martin never cared much for material things, houses or cars or other luxuries. He didn't rob for the money. We never had a flashy lifestyle. Family vacations consisted of nothing more glamorous than going to the UK to visit relatives. Even after the suspicious fire that engulfed the kitchen in Cowper

Downs, it never occurred to him to take out house insurance. Nothing he ever had was covered by insurance, except for the compulsory motor insurance, and even then he found it extremely difficult to get motor insurance for his cars and next to impossible for his motorbikes. Once he gave his name and address, most companies declined to offer him insurance. He couldn't get a passport because no garda would sign and stamp his application form. My brothers and I had tremendous difficulty in getting a passport, but with the help of Labour TD Ruairi Quinn I finally managed to get one when I was eighteen, after years of badgering the gardaí. My father didn't bother with the passport business and said he'd never get up in a plane anyway, as he preferred boats. 'At least you have a bit of wood to hang onto if it sinks,' he'd say. He liked to keep his feet firmly planted on the ground.

*

Martin's temper would flare up at times, totally unexpected and unpredictable. One time, while the family was sitting around the table eating dinner in the kitchen, he was unusually quiet. He stood up, walked into the hall and went slowly up the stairs. We looked at each other; my mother looked a little nervous. Then, for no apparent reason, he began smashing each picture with his fist as he walked past the pictures that were lined up on the wall. The sound of the glass smashing seemed to go on for ages. My mother just rolled her eyes in disapproval. We carried on with our meal and nobody said a word when he returned. I later learned that he had backed his motorbike into a wall and smashed the rear light; his frustration was taken out on the pictures in the hall.

Martin had diabetes, so he couldn't tolerate excessive amounts of sugar. He didn't need to inject insulin, but the diabetes wreaked havoc on him all the same. Sometimes when he ate chocolate he suffered terrible headaches and he would get irritable and his temper could flare up. He dealt with it by going to bed and sleeping until the pain in his head left him. The media wrongly portrayed him as a cream cake-guzzling glutton. This was in stark contrast to the reality that he was always highly conscious of his sugar intake. In fact, he was actually quite health conscious, and always had been throughout his life. As a young man he was a keep fit enthusiast, almost to the point of being fanatical. When he got older, the diabetes, which was hereditary, slowed him down, but he never drank alcohol or smoked. He didn't drink sugary fizzy drinks and his appetite was generally quite small.

He did enjoy Chinese food, though, and would take my mother out to the Chinese restaurant in Ranelagh every now and again. He really liked the staff there, who were always welcoming and pleasant and drinks were always on the house. He thought the

Chinese people were the nicest people he had ever met. He told them if they were ever having any problems, they could come to him any time.

*

My father also helped a lot of the family set up businesses. He wanted us to make an honest living. He had a great interest in having a business that would bring the family a regular income, especially after his dole payments were cut off after the **Today Tonight** programme. The police would always try to put a stop to any business venture he involved himself in. One of the first was a small snooker hall in Crumlin. It took off and started to get quite busy until the gardaí sat outside and warned all the customers to keep away from the place or they would be arrested. Other businesses he became involved with setting up were a couple of newsagents, a chip shop, a pub, a travel agent and, bizarrely, a cemetery. (He was in negotiations to buy Mount Jerome Cemetery in Harold's Cross, but he pulled out of it.) As usual, the gardaí would harass the business owners and intimidate the customers – anything to stop Martin Cahill earning an honest buck.

*

Martin's talents lay in many things, including his way of winning people over. He was very charismatic and everyone who knew him liked him. People who weren't that close had a certain fear of him, his reputation fuelled by stories such as the much-hyped tale of how he had nailed a friend of his who stole from him to the floor – or was it a snooker table, or did I see that in a movie once?

The true story is quite different. Someone robbed my father. An associate of Martin's – I will call him Mr L – had led Martin to believe that this guy O (again, not his real name) was the culprit. O was a loveable guy, one of the nice ones. Mr L told my father that O had stolen a consignment of gold from him – Mr L himself being the guilty party. O was questioned in relation to the missing gold by Martin, but Mr L hammered the nail in. The fella wasn't crucified, as popular tabloid and Hollywood make-believe have portrayed. Anyone that knew my father knew the real story – he didn't nail anyone to anything. I have always been amazed at the level of violence my father was supposedly capable of, when he could never even bring himself to cull his pigeons.

He was always squeamish in my eyes, even a bit of a wimp sometimes. We once had a dog, the type that had its tail foxed. When she had a litter of puppies, he couldn't bring himself to fox the puppies' tails. One of his friends came down and did the deed in our garage. The puppies were squealing and the mother, who could hear her puppies' cries, was very distressed. Martin held on to her, rubbing her head. His friend emerged with the handful of bloody tails and handed them to Martin, who shook his head. 'Jaysus, you're a sadistic bastard,' he said. His friend made a joke of it, but I knew my father couldn't have done it himself. Times like these showed a gentle side to my father, but it's true there was another side to him too.

Martin wasn't the type to go around terrorising people. He and his brothers just went out did whatever it was they had to do, then came home and patted the kids on the head. They didn't go around flexing their muscles – they left that to others who believed that instilling fear was the only way to get any respect. They were wrong. People rarely crossed my father. Rather, it was the unspoken word that generated a certain fear in people when it came to Martin. I could say with near certainty that he never actually had a physical fight with anybody in his life. Yet nobody ever messed with him, ever. He never had to resort to violence on a person. He hated bullies and he hated violence. It was something he always tried to avoid.

He told me that one night he was out mooching about and saw the gardaí at the top of the road, so he had to duck into a garden for a few minutes, just until the law passed. He was standing behind a bush in the garden when he was spotted by the owner of the house. Martin waited for the inevitable confrontation. This man, who was over six feet tall and had rugby player shoulders, walked over to Martin, muttering, 'Get out of there. What the fuck are you doing in my garden?' He grabbed Martin by the shoulders. Martin didn't want to hit him and he didn't want to cause a loud commotion, not with the gardaí just yards away. Martin sprang up, got the fella in a tight headlock and quickly explained that he was Martin Cahill and he meant him no harm, he was just hiding in the garden for a couple of minutes until the gardaí passed. Martin wasn't as athletic as the other fella, but he was as strong as an ox and very quick. The fella realised who he was dealing with and quickly told Martin that it was fine, okay, no problem, and did he want to come in the house for a minute until they left?

He went in and sat down with the man, who made Martin a drop of tea. Martin thanked him for the tea and went on his way. On his way out, he invited him up to the house in Cowper Downs to a party that was being held that Saturday. He accepted, and sure enough, on the Saturday night, the guy showed up with his girlfriend. He and Martin remained friends until Martin died.

*

My father taught us to spot evil a mile off, be it a look, a gesture or an uncaring action – small actions give a person's character away. He couldn't abide rudeness or any form of cruelty towards children. One time at home, a couple of the kids were fighting and one of them slapped the other across the back, leaving a flat red handprint which stood out alarmingly on the white skin. Martin went berserk, sending the offending child out of the house and instructing him never to return if that was the way he was going to treat people. 'They may as well start their garda training now. They'll welcome you with open arms in Templemore if that's the way you want to treat people,' he said.

He recognised what was genuine and what was not and he tried damn hard to pass it on to his children. His intuition wore off on the family and proved itself when it had no choice but to surface.

*

My father was very protective of me and watched any boyfriend I had with an aloofness. I can best describe it as the typical father–daughter thing – he wanted a decent chap for his daughter. He would tease me about my boyfriend Mark and how we seemed to be getting serious about each other. He would always ask me to invite him over for dinner, but I was a little shy there, thinking my father would ask him silly questions and embarrass me – again, typical father–daughter things.

One night, there was a party at our house in Cowper Downs and a fight broke out amongst a couple of young people that showed up after having too much to drink. My father threw everyone out of the house that night. He pointed at Mark to get out too. Mark shrugged his shoulders and left. The next morning, myself and Dad were sitting at the breakfast table and he was saying, 'Ah, I think that's the last you'll be seeing of him, daughter. I don't think he will show his face around here again.' I pulled a face at him to be quiet. He patted me on the head, which got on my nerves.

The next thing, the doorbell rang and when I answered it, Mark stood there, smiling. We went up to my room and had a good laugh about the previous night. I told him my da didn't expect him to come back. He laughed again and asked, 'Why not?'

'Because he thought you would be rattling,' I said. We had another laugh at this.

After that, my father told me that I wouldn't meet a better fella than Mark. He was always impressed at the way Mark handled the gardaí – they would stop him coming into our estate and tell him to keep away from Frances Cahill, her father's a dangerous man and she's a prostitute. Mark would take the garda's name and tell them that he would be making a complaint at the local station. They would follow him home and sit outside his house, but Mark didn't mind. Even though he had never had any encounters with the gardaí in his life, he never showed any fear of them. My father had great respect for him because of this.

*

I asked my father a question not long before he died. I asked – no, I accused him – of not having a conscience. He turned to me with a puzzled look on his face and said, 'Conscience? About what? I have nothing on my conscience, why do you ask?'

I felt foolish then. Was I falling into the trap of making judgments about my father, the man who had done nothing but love us? He gave us everything he could, and most importantly, he gave us himself. He was always there for his children, no matter what. His love was unconditional. He raised us to never judge, to never come to conclusions about people on face value alone and to accept that everyone is unique – you just have to cop on quickly to the bad ones. I felt I had let him down, but he could see I regretted it as soon as I said it and he forgave me. He overlooked small mistakes as long as he could see in your eyes that you knew you were wrong.

— Part III
End of an Era

Chapter 10
Que Sera, Sera

Living with the knowledge that your life was in immense and increasing danger, waiting for a bullet to end it all at any moment, would certainly have a person on edge. But not my father.

Martin had been receiving warnings about his imminent death for months. The first one came in the post on his birthday, 23 May 1994. Expecting a birthday card, he opened the post while we were gathered around the kitchen table, drinking tea and slagging him for being an old man; he was only forty-five. He read the letter, smiled and threw it down amongst the sugar bowl and mugs.

'What do ye think of that?' he asked my mother.

She picked it up and read it aloud. He had a smile on his face as she read: 'Martin Cahill, this is a warning, please take it seriously. Your life is in danger. You will be shot dead within the next few months. Do not treat this as a joke.'

I looked at him. He raised his eyebrows in that familiar way and laughed quietly.

'What?' he said to me.

'Are you gonna take this seriously, Da?' I asked. My mother just stood there with the letter crumpled in her fist.

'Ah Jaysus, if I was to take everything serious in life, I'd be a looney,' he replied.

'You are a looney, Da, and forty-five. It's the old folks' home for ye next!' I laughed and watched as my mother tightened her fist around the paper and quickly threw it in the bin.

*

That was the first of a total of five warnings he received before his murder in August 1994. I didn't know he got any more until after he died. My mother said that with each one he would just laugh and shrug it off, telling her not to worry about things like that, he'd got stuff like that for years. His routine didn't change and he never showed any sign of nervousness. In fact, he seemed happier than ever. He was eagerly awaiting the birth of my first child and life was good. He did have a lot on his mind, but then, he always did. A few death threats would not – could not – faze him.

A week before he died, my father and I were in the living room at Cowper Downs watching television when a knock came to the door. My brother Martin Jr. answered it. We could hear voices and my father nodded to me to go and see who it was, but before I could get to the door, Martin was already closing it.

'Who was that?' my father asked, but Martin Jr. looked a little puzzled and shrugged his shoulders.

'Some fella asked me the time when I opened the door, so I went in the kitchen to see and when I came back out he was gone.'

My father was furious. 'Don't be leaving the door open! Be careful who you open the door to!' He was agitated over this, something we had never seen in him before. I believe he was afraid someone would come into the house and shoot him in front of us; he would not have wanted us to go through that.

*

Many sinister people had tried and failed to form a friendship with Martin. The connection was usually made through a close friend or a friend of a friend, but one such person tried another way to worm his way into my father's company. This person took the unlikely form of a Catholic priest.

My father received a postcard from Disneyworld in Florida from a priest who was eager to meet him. He hoped to come to our house and 'have a chat'. Intrigued, Martin agreed to a meeting. I'm sure the Disney connection was to grab my father's attention, but he found the idea of having a priest as an acquaintance quite amusing, so he went along with it.

The priest visited the house, but this fellow was not your average priest. It turned out he had a coloured past which led to him being banned from Northern Ireland – he was a gun runner for the IRA. He was one of the most evil-looking people to have ever set foot inside our home and I disliked him immediately. When I asked my father what was the story with your man, he laughed and said, 'Ah well, at least if anything happens to me while he's around, he can give me the last rites.'

I knew Martin regarded this priest as a joke and he tired of him very quickly. We were instructed to tell him my father wasn't home when he called unexpectedly. He wasn't around on the day my father was killed, but he showed up the day after. He sat on our sofa and I watched him suspiciously. His eyes darted around the room and he stared at each caller to the house. We never saw him again after that day, but a couple of weeks later I came across an article in one of the papers saying he was being allowed back into Northern Ireland. I couldn't help but wonder what it was he had done for them to allow him the freedom of the border crossing.

*

I awoke on Thursday, 18 August 1994 to the gentle sound of my child stirring in her basket. I had given birth two weeks previously to my first child, a beautiful baby girl. She was my father's second grandchild. The sun threatened to break through a few clouds that had gathered overhead and I rose out of bed to attend to my daughter. I was planning to take her for a walk later, but after breakfast I had some errands to run in Rathmines.

Having a child threw a whole new perspective on life. I was very proud of myself and my father was very proud of us. I can still see his face when he walked into the ward in the Coombe maternity hospital. I was holding my baby as he walked in. I watched his eyes, followed them across the room. He didn't lose eye contact with me – he didn't look at the baby. His face was flushed with joy and pride as he reached my bedside. His first words were, 'Are you okay?' I was still a child to him; his child. I was twenty-four.

I tucked a blanket around my baby's legs, put the seatbelt over the car seat and set off down the Rathmines Road. I went to a local shopping centre and bought a toy for my cousin Billy's birthday. He was three years old that day and the rest of the family had all gone to his party in a nearby amusement centre. I didn't go because I thought my baby was too young for all the noise. My mother had gone with her two sisters and a gang of kids. They would be back around four o'clock and I was to meet them in my mother's house in Swan Grove. My father had stayed there that night and I was hoping to catch him before he left.

I left the shopping centre around quarter to four and headed down towards Ranelagh. I could see the garda squad car blocking the road ahead and heard police sirens in the distance, then another squad car whizzed past me, heading towards Ranelagh. Something was going on.

When I reached the roadblock, I cursed the garda blocking my way, as I had to go all the way around the canal and back up towards Ranelagh to reach Swan Grove. When I finally got around, there was another roadblock and the gardaí on duty were chatting excitedly to each other, laughing amongst themselves and getting on my nerves.

I lowered my window and shouted to one of them, 'What the hell is going on? Why are the roads blocked?' I got no reply and was waved on to go ahead for local access.

When I arrived at Swan Grove, neighbours were standing around talking in small groups, and when I passed they all stared at my car. They were obviously talking about me and they looked very serious.

I pulled up outside our house and took the baby's car seat out of the car. Three or four women that had gathered across the road called me over. I had a feeling there was something wrong.

The first thing one of them said was, 'How's the baby?' but she didn't smile as you would expect. I replied that she was fine, then I asked if there was something wrong.

One of them stepped closer to me. 'There's been an accident. It's your da.'

Immediately, I said, 'Where is he? What's happened? Is he hurt?'

'We heard he was ... dead,' she replied. A feeling of dread crept over me. Everything started to appear as if in slow motion – the woman's lips kept moving, but I couldn't hear the words. I was feeling dizzy. Out of the corner of my eye, I saw my mother's car pull up slowly behind my car. My mother stepped out. I saw her mouth form the words 'What's wrong?' but I couldn't hear a sound.

One of the neighbours ran to her to tell her. I wanted to reach her first to stop this woman from telling her, but my feet felt like lead. I couldn't get to her fast enough. I saw her raise her hands to her head and her face screwed up in pain. (I later learned that my mother had heard of her husband's death over the radio as she arrived at the house that day. The media didn't even have the decency to wait until his family had been informed.)

Suddenly, everything went very fast. We were inside the house and I started to scream. My mother was in a panic. All around us, everyone started to cry. The children were beginning to realise what had happened and they started to cry. I kept shouting at my mother, 'What's happened? What's happened?'

She said, 'He's been shot, but he's not dead, he's not dead!' I could hardly believe what I was hearing.

'Where is he? Call a fucking ambulance! The police have him, they will let him die. Where is he?' My baby started to cry with all the commotion and my mother took her from me. I left the house and ran down the road towards Ranelagh. I could see the road blocked ahead and a crowd of people and garda cars had gathered at the scene. The gardaí had cordoned off the area and weren't letting anybody through.

I saw his van, a small black Renault 5, covered in clear plastic, with a grotesque red blanket covering the wind screen. The car had crashed into a railing at the far side of the road and had come to a halt on the opposite footpath. Police were holding back the crowd of onlookers. I approached one of the guards. 'That's my father's van,' I said. He looked at me, expressionless. 'Is he dead?' I asked. The garda nodded his head and smiled.

I ran back towards the house in Swan Grove. I had to do something – there was no ambulance at the scene and I was worried that he was injured inside the car and needed medical attention. The police weren't letting anybody in and I was worried that if he was still alive, they were just waiting for him to die in the car. I had to get someone in there that could see if he was really dead.

I ran into a shop that had a pay phone and frantically searched through the phone directory for Gareth Sheehan's number. I got him and asked him to come down to the scene in Ranelagh and see if my father was dead or injured. He had to come quickly – he could be dying as we spoke. I hung up the phone and tried to think of what to do next. Maybe he was hurt and had been taken to a hospital before I got there. My mind was racing. I was in a complete panic. I decided to get down to the nearest hospital to see if they had him. I ran to my car, which was back at the house. My youngest brother, Luke, who was aged seven, ran up to me. He was crying.

'They're all sayin' Da's dead, Fran. Is Da dead?' He looked at me and I held his face in my hands.

'Don't worry, Luke, it's all right. I'm going to find out what's happening. You go inside to Ma now.' I saw my older brother, Martin Jr., walking towards the house. His face was white and he looked confused and in shock. Luke ran to him and Martin took his hand.

'Martin, I'm going down to the hospitals. You go down to Ranelagh – don't take Luke!' I shouted. I drove quickly to the Meath hospital and ran into the emergency room. A nurse stopped me and asked if I was okay.

'Was someone taken in with gunshot wounds?' I pleaded.

She looked confused. 'Now, who is it you're looking for?'

I was frantic. I started to run through the emergency ward, looking behind each curtain to see if he was there.

The nurse grabbed my arm. 'Now look, what is it you're looking for?' she repeated.

I ran out the hospital door back to my car and drove back to the house. Mr Sheehan was on the scene very quickly. He went down to the van to see what was going on. I waited at the house for him to come back. The minutes dragged by and I felt dizzy and nauseous, my head spinning.

Gareth knocked hard on the door and when I opened it, he was quite pale and spoke very softly. 'I'm sorry. He's gone, he's died.'

'No,' I replied very matter of factly. 'Are you sure? The gardaí are probably only saying that. They are letting him die.' I started to get upset and panicky.

'No, Frances, I saw him myself. He's gone. There's nothing we can do now. I'm very sorry,' he shook his head.

I thanked Gareth and gently closed the door.

*

We watched the six o'clock news and sat there staring quietly at the screen as they carried his body, which was in a black body bag, to the waiting hearse. People began to arrive at the house. My mother paced the floors. I looked over at Luke. His little face was blotched red from crying but he was quiet now. He looked over at me.

'Fran, what about his pigeons? Who's going to look after the pigeons?'

I gave him a little smile. 'Don't worry about it now, Luke. Don't worry.' I gave him a hug.

'Ah, I'll do it. Me and Chris will do it,' he said bravely. I quickly wiped the tears from his face that had begun to fall once again. Luke wasn't seven any more. He was a little man now.

*

Dublin City Morgue is a bleak, dreary building in a soulless part of the city. One could feel the bitter heartache felt by those unfortunate enough to have to visit this vile place in the past. It has a surgical stench which clings to its black and grey walls.

My mother, my father's sister Teresa and I were huddled together in the waiting area. The waiting area is in a small courtyard, wide open to the elements, with a small shelter for people to get out of the rain and have a cigarette. We stood under the shelter and the dim light threw a ghastly shadow of us onto the ground. My mother took long, slow drags from her cigarette, which had burned right down to her fingers. Her hands shook. We waited for someone to come and call us. They told us that they had my father's body inside and my mother would have to identify it. Her voice broke the deadly silence. She kept repeating, over and over, 'It's not him. It's not him. He is hiding somewhere, I just know it. He is watching everything and laughing.'

'Do you think so?' Teresa asked. She looked at me and shook her head. I knew not to open my mouth.

A man came out. 'Frances Cahill,' he said, 'come this way please.'

I took my mother's hand and told her she didn't have to do it. 'She does, Fran, she does,' Teresa said. 'I will go in with her, she won't be alone.'

They went in and I was left there by myself. My legs started to shake uncontrollably and I could hear my teeth chattering in my head.

Just one minute later, my mother rushed through the morgue doors and went past me, followed by Teresa, who was sobbing.

'Is it him?' I asked, hoping for some sort of miracle. My mother just looked at me and said, 'Oh my God, get me out of here!'

One of my father's friends was outside with a car and we left immediately. We piled into the car and Teresa told him to go. The car drove off quickly, speeding down towards the quays. I turned to Teresa, who looked shocked, and asked her what he looked like. 'Asleep, he looked asleep,' she replied.

*

His funeral was surreal. People were all around us and there was no escape from the masses of faces. I had seen him the day before, lying in his coffin. I had seen dead people before, but never one that really did look asleep. I had seen him stretched out on the sofa a million times looking the same as he did now, though I had never looked so closely as I did that day. I had never noticed how thick and long his dark eyelashes were. He was wearing a waistcoat he'd had since the 1960s – his lucky waistcoat, he called it – and a tie I had bought him the previous Father's Day, a cartoon Mickey Mouse tie he liked. I remember him saying, 'Ah, you love me really, don't you, daughter?' He was always teasing me about that, always saying, 'You love your aul' da, don't you?' I never said I did. We weren't that type of family. I'd just laugh and say, 'Yeah, sure. Sure I do.'

Before they closed the coffin, everyone in the room surged forward to touch him to say one last goodbye. I put a photograph of us, his wife and children, into his hand, gave him a kiss and said, 'Bye, Da. You just keep laughing at them all. Just keep laughing.' The lid was closed.

Outside the funeral parlour, hundreds of photographers had gathered across the road. One gentleman that worked there took my family out the back way so we wouldn't have to face the crowd of photographers. Nobody suggested this to him – he was just being kind. They didn't really bother us as such; they were just more faces. A garda escort stopped the traffic and waved the hearse through red lights. I sat in the car behind the hearse and watched the garda lower his head as my father's coffin passed. I didn't mind that the gardaí were around. They were only trying to annoy us, but it was not possible – had never been possible – especially now.

At the graveside, we had to push our way through the throngs of people gathered around the grave. Some of them were there out of morbid curiosity, but most were friends and family. The smell of the flowers was overwhelming. What seemed like hundreds of elaborate bouquets and wreaths went past me and were laid on the dirt. I felt sick with the cloying smell of the flowers and covered my mouth with my hand.

I detested the smell of flowers for a long time afterwards. Suddenly, a guitar started playing and everyone started to sing 'Que Sera, Sera', his favourite. It was comforting. My spirits were lifted slightly, but not for long.

*

I had just returned from the Terenure garda station, where my brother Chris and I had gone to get my father's car, the one that lay up in their yard riddled with bullet holes. There was no way we were leaving it up there a second longer for all of the coppers to gloat over and have their pictures taken beside. Funnily enough, I felt no more animosity towards them then than I had at any other time in my life.

I walked towards the car and climbed into the driver's seat. I put my hands on the steering wheel. The keys were in the ignition and I turned it. The battery was dead. We managed to push it out of the yard. When we passed one of the guards, he said, 'Take care now!' I ignored him and Christopher didn't look at him.

We continued down Terenure Road. I was afraid to look down. I didn't want to see the inside of the car. I kept my eyes fixed on the road ahead and glanced at Christopher in the wing mirror. A look of relief was on his face and I knew he felt the same as I did. We had taken back a piece of my father.

We brought the car to a lock-up in the KCR industrial estate. When we were leaving, I looked at the car then. It looked so sad, so broken and empty, like a huge hand had grabbed it and shaken it violently until it started to bleed and die. It looked like death.

I stood in the bathroom back at the house and stared into the mirror. I hadn't cried. My father had been dead for two weeks and I couldn't cry. I looked down at my hands and brought them closer to my face. Underneath my fingernails was caked with blood. I squinted and looked closer. In between the lines of my palms were flakes of dried blood. I scrubbed furiously at my fingernails and tried to block the sight of the broken glass, the bullet holes, the thick, black, dried blood on the steering wheel from my mind. There was a loud screaming in my head, but it stopped as I watched the last of my father's blood go down the drain.

*

It wasn't until two weeks after the funeral that I was showed the mail: hundreds of letters of condolence, some from as far away as Australia. Some of the mail was hateful, people telling us how bad our father was, people who had never met him but of course had their own opinions on him. We would just flick the letter in the bin. 'That's from another copper,' we'd say.

*

When my father was killed, one of the first things I thought was how helpless he was, unable to cover his face when he lay dead in his little car. The detectives on the scene could take advantage of the fact that he was gone to get a good long look. But he was just that – gone – and nothing they did now mattered. He wasn't at their mercy; he never was.

The journalists on the scene criticised the gardaí for not allowing them to photograph the 'slain General'. Make no mistake – some senior members of the force would have liked nothing more than to have seen his blood all over the tabloids. I feel for others whose fathers or loved ones have been murdered and then had to endure the pain of seeing the image of their loved one splashed over the pages of some hideous newspaper.

Far from the media interest ending after my father's death, it became more intense. Even now, the press will mention him any time there's an opportunity. Martin Cahill still sells papers.

*

The police later issued a statement that there was no surveillance on Martin Cahill the day he was shot. But are we really meant to believe that after watching him for years, they just decided to stop, that day of all days? My family believes the surveillance didn't stop – it never stopped – and it certainly didn't stop on the 18th of August, 1994.

*

For many months after my father's death, people would make suggestions to my mother as to who the culprits were and what they would have done to them. My mother would look at them hopelessly through tired, red eyes and shake her head; it was the last thing she wanted to think about. Each passing day, as callers stopped coming and the house grew quieter, I would sit in the living room listening to her pottering around quietly and sighing heavily. Now and again we would hold our breaths momentarily when we heard the front door open and close, footsteps coming up the hall, then let out a deep sigh when one of my brothers or an uncle would come in. It's a strange feeling to expect a person who's dead to suddenly just walk into the room, but it's one that stays with you for a very long time.

My father's wardrobe was still full of his clothes. His jackets and trousers hung there, each telling their own story as I gently pushed the hangers back. I found the Mickey Mouse T-shirt he'd worn for his trouser-dropping stunt lying in a crumpled heap under a couple of shirts. I picked it up and smiled.

*

When my daughter was born on 3 August 1994, my father insisted that I call her after myself, like my own mother had done with me. I wanted to call her Eve, and that was her name until Martin's death, just two weeks after her birth. I felt compelled then to call his granddaughter what my father wanted her to be named.

Since my father's death, he has never been far from my thoughts. As with most people who have experienced such loss, you never quite recover from the pain that engulfs you. However, it is true that as time passes you remember the good times and tend to recall pleasurable experiences more often than painful ones. And you accept your loved one's death – you come to terms with it. To quote my father, 'What will be, will be.' He would say this to focus us, to ground us. In his familiar, calm tone, he would reassure us that you must accept what life throws at you, deal with it and be strong.

I can still see him now.

Accepting my father's death was an extremely hard thing for us to do. He was so full of life, so different. He was good, he was strange, he was complex, he was charismatic, he was fun, he could smile and laugh at himself and others.

He was my father.

What more can I say?

Chapter 11
Keep Smiling

Martin always knew that they would shoot him dead in the end. From that day in the field at the age of ten to the day the gardaí planted a firearm in his toilet, he knew they couldn't stand not being able to get the better of him. He knew they couldn't catch him doing anything. They didn't have the power to frame him – he could see them from all directions and he would continue to fight back until his dying day. They knew he would never give in. He stood up to them and kept on hitting back, no matter what. There was no one in Ireland the establishment hated more.

Many Irish detectives' entire careers revolved around catching Martin Cahill. They firmly believed that he and his gang were responsible for many armed robberies carried out in the republic, for this was another label they attached to him – he was a 'crime boss', the brains behind all his daring robberies. He was put in a box and tagged a criminal. What was it about him that made members of the gardaí believe without a shadow of a doubt that he carried out all the crimes they ascribed to him? Was he clever? Cunning? Beyond reach? What?

He learned from a young age that no one was going to help you when you come from poverty. He and his brothers were expected to be nothing more than dole fodder. They answered back when they were kids and fought back as adults.

But what he was – what he became – wasn't really him; it was what they turned him into. He wasn't born an armed robber. He wasn't born with a chip on his shoulder. What he really was, was a man who knew society for what it was. He knew what being Irish was all about. He knew how the police worked; he could always predict their next move. He understood the corruption and the deviousness of the Irish establishment.

We Irish are very hard to understand. In one era, we turn our heads and say a quiet prayer when we see a Christian Brother beat a child with a leather strap and give helpless young boys a flogging the likes of which was last seen on African slave ships, and then in another era we re-elect corrupt politicians as prisoners are tortured in their cells, their human rights smashed to smithereens, while we, the public, turn a blind eye. Children are dying in police custody and we shrug our shoulders. We bite our lip and say nothing when the Americans use us as lapdogs as we allow them to use our airports for military stopovers, giving them a cheerful Irish wave as they continue on towards their deadly missions into the east.

Martin knew who the real criminals are in this country – the corrupt politicians and the abusive religious orders. He saw a blind eye being turned to the abusive middle classes. He saw that money means more than most anything else. A child's life means very little in this country, as was proven in the Robert Houlihan case. The abuse that boys and girls suffered at the hands of the religious orders who were meant to care for and nurture them is unforgivable. And it doesn't end – it runs on and on into the future. Martin tried to let the authorities know that he knew. He didn't hide his opinions, he literally shouted them from the rooftop, and the gardaí sat there, seething.

*

Yes, Martin Cahill hated authority. He despised the hypocrisy of the Church and the whole establishment An Garda Síochána, with its corruption and ruthlessness. He always believed the truth would come out about the Irish police force one day – and it has.

Some say Martin single-handedly illustrated the need for a major overhaul of the absolute right to silence. He was well known and despised by the gardaí as a person who could not be forced to give up his right to silence. He would pick a point on the wall and stare at it, chanting to himself, 'I have nothing to say to you,' over and over again. Certainly, exercising his right to silence saved him from the inevitable – being framed by a system that despised him.

Police corruption has made the news in recent years, from the Kerry Babies case to the Morris Tribunal findings, with reports of ill treatment by the gardaí even drawing the attention of Amnesty International. Meanwhile, fourteen-year-old Brian Rossiter was found unconscious in his cell while in garda custody and died a few days later in 2002, while in 2005, twenty-year-old Terence Wheelock hung himself in his cell, dying three months later after never regaining consciousness.

Society should be beating down the doors of garda cells and demanding that all garda station interrogation cells and holding rooms have recording CCTV cameras installed immediately. The gardaí themselves should make this demand – surely they would want protection against any accusations?

My father was criminalised from the age of ten for a minor offence. Today, this is being done through the widespread use of Anti-Social Behaviour Orders (ASBOs). Many young people stand to be tagged as criminals, when sometimes the only 'crime' they've committed is standing in the wrong place at the wrong time. Society should worry now, not complain in fifteen years' time when the crime rate is at an all-time high thanks to the direction that a person with an ASBO is inevitably heading. Educate, don't label.

Yet Martin was far from anti-establishment. He believed in people working hard for what they wanted in life, but he hated stepping on people to get there.

He did what he could to survive and he loved his family. One of his biggest achievements was being a father. No one could take that away from him.

And yet, they tried to demonise him. They screamed and ranted about how the public couldn't sleep easy at night with the likes of Martin Cahill prowling around. He had to be stopped!

*

It was strange after my father died. Everything stopped; the surveillance, the harassment. Life became normal, which was hard for us to get used to at first. Suddenly we were just like everyone else.

My mother is now living her life back in her native Dublin after a short spell in the UK after her husband's death. She is glad to have returned to Ireland and is now working for a charity, working with alcoholic people who have nothing but the streets. She works in a 'wet house', the only intervention between real life and despair for alcoholics on the street, feeding them, cleaning them and giving them some shred of dignity. I always knew that caring for others would eventually become her role in life. Her unselfish attitude towards these people is a credit to her and her children are all extremely proud of her strength and courage. She matched my father in every way – always the individual.

Gareth Sheehan, Martin's lifelong solicitor who often went out of his way to help, has now been made an Irish court judge.

Eddie Cahill is now a successful, renowned artist, exhibiting his work across Europe and beyond, committed to his art. Mary Robinson came to one of his shows. He is simply an inspiration and a winner in all of our eyes.

Martin's remaining living family are well and living in Dublin. The Cahill family were all together at a recent family gathering in 2007. I looked around at them all, most of them the image of Martin. The sun was shining and we were all glad to be together after all these years. Everyone was there – John, Eddie, Michael, Gerard, Mary, Una, Teresa, Ann, Angie, cousins and friends. Everyone was smiling and carefree. My aul' fella would have loved to have been there. They came out the other end and they came out smiling, just like he once told reporters after one of his court appearances: 'Keep on smiling, that's what it's all about.' I felt an overwhelming amount of achievement for them.

And there wasn't a garda car in sight.

*

Once the authorities had Martin tagged, he couldn't shake it, so he made a conscious decision instead – if they said he was a criminal, then by God, he was going to be the biggest criminal, the biggest thorn in their sides. He would make them regret their choice.

They should have left him alone on that wall, diving into the grass with his friends, with his dreams of becoming a sailor. Maybe, just maybe, all of his dreams could have come true. For in the end, they never got their medals. They never got Martin, they never ruined him. He would always be that innocent boy at age ten.

As for all the other stuff in his life, the whole whirlwind of it, all I can say now, in the words of my father, is: 'Live now, you're a long time dead!' His love of life and his love for his family are what we will always remember him for. No one can ever take that away from us.